REDLANDS – OUR TOWN

REDLANDS

OUR TOWN

by
FRANK E. MOORE

with sketches by
JEFF OWENS

MOORE HISTORICAL FOUNDATION
REDLANDS, CALIFORNIA
1987

Library of Congress Catalog Card Number 87-61972

ISBN 0-914167-05-7 soft cover
ISBN 0-914167-04-9 hard cover

Copyright © 1987 by Frank E. Moore

OTHER MOORE HISTORICAL FOUNDATION BOOKS

Redlands Yesterdays, a Photo Album, 1870–1920 by William G. Moore, 1983.
(Out of print)

Redlands, Impressions by Leo Politi, 1983. $15.00
Paintings of Redlands Mansions

Two Girls and a Kite or Adventures Around the Kite Shaped Track
by Edith Parker (Hinckley), 1984. $12.50
Southern California seen from Santa Fe RR 1899

With a Grain of Salt by Frank E. Moore, 1985. $15.00
A collection of Mr. Moore's newspaper columns from *Redlands Daily Facts.*

Fun With Fritz compiled by William G. Moore, 1986, $20.00
Adventures in early Redlands, Big Bear, and Hollywood
with John H. "Fritz" Fisher.

MOORE HISTORICAL FOUNDATION
300 East State Street, Suite 506
Redlands, California 92373
Phone (714) 798-2403

Contents

Preface

IN PREPARING to write *Redlands – Our Town* my first decision was this: "I will not reinvent the wheel. I will not write still another general history, merely picking up the story where others left off.

"Rather, I will leave to others the concept that the history of Redlands is a continuum, an unbroken series of events, one linked to another like a chain."

The reality, in my view, is that there was an *Old* Redlands and now there is a *New* Redlands. The break between them came in 1942. It was sharp.

Redlands I was citrus-centered. The orange shaped the town and dominated it.

Redlands II was brought into being by Adolph Hitler. He attacked Poland in September 1939; World War II was underway. President Roosevelt declared a limited national emergency. It became inevitable that the United States would raise a great military force and enter the war.

That caused Norton Air Force Base to be established just outside Redlands. Thousands of civilians were hired. An influx of new population began. The die was cast. The demand for more and more housing would continue indefinitely. Tracts replaced groves. Citrus declined in acreage and collapsed in influence.

Redlands II is primarily a residential city. The largest single employer of our people is the U.S. Air Force. Reminding everyone of this are the cargo jets that constantly take off over the town.

The radical transformation of Redlands I into Redlands II is explained in the latter parts of this book, especially in the final section, "Tides of Change."

Entirely different in character is the opening section, "Setting the Scene." This deals with the givens, the constants, the verities of Redlands.

Exactly where is Our Town on the globe? What is the weather that made Redlands an ideal place for growing navel oranges? What is the mystique of our mountains, touching the very souls of our people? Do you live near a fault? (Yes.) And the beauty that is here to enjoy, in the trees, in the delicate clouds and in the starry sky.

Why did I choose to write about these particular things? Because I have learned about them from experience, as so many long-term residents have. Additionally, I was a Redlands news-paperman for nearly 50 years and in line of duty paid close attention to various things, such as the weather. In the main, I have written about what I know about.

The second section, "Getting to Know Redlands," should help new residents become familiar with the sights, the land-marks and the street names. Oldtimers, too, may be stimulated to take notice of interesting things that have always escaped their attention. The bibliography of books about the valley and the town should be especially helpful to those who wish to learn more about the place where they live.

In the third section, "History à la Carte," I attempt to explain several modern phenomena by delving into their histories. These topics are as different in nature as sports and the University of Redlands.

The perceptive reader will notice that I regard the automobile as the most powerful force in the physical development of the city, scattering our homes, our churches, our businesses. It has reshaped Our Town. Redlands I was agricultural; Redlands II is suburban. Commuters have replaced orange growers.

The automobile is a frequent topic in *Redlands – Our Town*, but not the subject of a chapter of its own.

Acknowledgements

THIS BOOK has been two years in the making. In that time countless people—perhaps as many as 150—have helped me in one
way or another. No one ever refused to answer a question
whether over the telephone, face-to-face, or in an hour-long
interview. Indeed, everyone seemed to enjoy participating in
"Our Town."

I wish I could name them all but I think you will agree that
such a roster would be unduly long. So I will limit my specific
thanks to the following:

—The late Steve Nicks for his sharp insight into the decline of
citrus.

—Corrine Bromberger for her knowledge of Redlands ornamental trees and John Hiatt for his remarkable inventory of our
street trees.

—Obrey Brown, a fountain of information about Redlands
sports.

—Kay Beattie for the correct account of her father's service as
the first teacher in present-day Redlands.

—Bill Schindler, former city planning director, for his vast
knowledge of planning, preservation and growth.

—Lorrie Poyzer, city clerk, for checking Council records, and
Bob Dale, building department head, for access to building
permits.

I am indebted to four friends for reading manuscript chapters, in their respective fields:

—Weather, Ron Hamilton, chief of the Agricultural Weather
Service.

—Faults and Earthquakes, Floyd Williams, consulting geologist and professor of geology.

—The chapter, "Doctors on the Move," Dr. Gordon Witter.

—Jet aircraft over Redlands, Wayne Mishak, retired aircraft
controller.

Although I never met Thornton Wilder, who died in 1975, it was his delightful 1938 play, *Our Town,* that suggested just the right title for this book. I talked with others and pondered a title for two years before the final name crystallized.

For the production aspects of this book, I am indebted to:

— Dick West, for editing the manuscript. He made 1,200 corrections in punctuation and spelling, and gave me his wise counsel.

— My brother, Bill, and my wife, Sidney, for proofreading.

— "Monty" Montaño for indexing.

— Mrs. Elva Marshall of The Castle Press for skillful design and layout of the book.

— The Moore Foundation and its founder, my brother, Bill, for constant encouragement and for making publication possible.

Perhaps I owe the most of all to Jeff Owens, the talented Redlands artist, for undertaking the illustration of the book with enthusiasm and understanding. Surely his sketches illuminate the pages and explain many things that the text could not.

Jeff is also responsible for the eye-catching art on the soft cover and the jacket.

FRANK E. MOORE

*To permanently enrich the community of Redlands is
the aim of many citizens in the Centennial period, 1987–88.
This book is my personal contribution.*
FRANK E. MOORE

1
SETTING THE
REDLANDS SCENE

'I Come from Redlands'

To ANSWER THE QUESTION that every Redlander is asked when he travels, let's imagine a conversation. The men are Geoffrey Allen, a British journalist, and Frank Moore. By chance they are seatmates on an airliner flying from London to Los Angeles.

Geoffrey: Where are you from?

Frank: Southern California.

G: Why "Southern"? Do you have a north and south like the Dakotas, the states we just flew over?

F: No, California is one state politically. But the people who live there don't think of it that way. The people in the North are absolutely paranoid about us. They are sure we are going to steal their water. You would think we were horse thieves in the Old West the way they talk about us.

G: What's the problem?

F: The water is in the North, but the greater population is in the South. Los Angeles has always gone after the water wherever it happened to be. It's no wonder the folks north of Tehachapi are a bit nervous.

G: But you didn't tell me the name of your city.

F: It's "Redlands," although the locals say the name as if it were spelled Red-lunds. I went to your country a year after the Great Train Robbery. United Press had reported some of the loot was found in The Redlands. So, of course, I had to see it. As you know, it's a forested mountain with a grand view but no city.

G: Is there any other reason you said "Southern California"?

F: Yes, but it's a rather humiliating subject. When an American—say he is from Chicago—asks where I am from I say "Redlands, California." Nine times out of ten he will be rather

3

vague, at first, and then he will say, "That's up in northern California, isn't it?"

He is talking about Redding which, as you notice, has a similar sound. As far as I know, Redding is just an ordinary city, although important as a county seat and a commercial center.

G: I don't understand. Why do they know Redding but not Redlands?

F: That puzzled me for years, but I think I finally know the answer. If we are vague about distant places, we usually know the names of the primary cities. We are weak on the locations of the secondary cities and suburbs. Every American knows of London but most of them do not know that Greenwich is a suburb. In our region, San Bernardino is the primary city; Redlands is a secondary city.

G: When you direct their attention to Southern California as the location of Redlands, do they then become clear?

F: Well, I can almost hear the gears and wheels going around in their heads as they try to retrieve whatever information may be stored in their memories. Do you know what they say? They say, "There is a college, or university or something there, isn't there?"

It's a curious fact that people often have a consciousness of the University of Redlands but not of the city in which it is located. This would disappoint the boosters who induced the Baptists to locate in Redlands in 1907. Part of the bargain was that the name of the school would include the name of the town.

G: Then you are content to let the University stand for the identification of Redlands? Perhaps some Americans who have never been to England are unaware that there is a city of Oxford at Oxford University and Cambridge at Cambridge University.

F: I used to tell them that "Redlands is an orange-growing, college and residential town, about halfway between Los Angeles and Palm Springs." Now I say that "Redlands used to be an orange-growing center but many of the groves have been pulled out. We are becoming a bedroom community. We have a college in town and a big Air Force base near by."

G: You've brought up a number of subjects. What's the orange story?

F: Now you are getting down to basic geography. There are high mountains — 10,000 feet, and higher — east of Redlands. They wring the moisture out of our storms and it flows down into our valley in the Santa Ana River. This river flows down through Riverside and Orange counties to the sea at Newport Beach.

A series of agricultural communities were founded along the Santa Ana. Disappointed gold seekers established the first one, near the coast. They called it Anaheim. You probably know of it because Disneyland is there.

The climate proved to be excellent for oranges. The Santa Ana became the "string" on which "beads" were strung — Santa Ana, Orange, Corona, Riverside, Redlands.

G: But if the Santa Ana was such an excellent place for oranges, why are they pulling out the orchards?

F: Because it has become more profitable to sell the land to a subdivider at a high price than to keep on farming it. The root of the matter is that the population of the United States keeps on growing — natural increase and immigration. Millions of people get tired of the cold in the East and migrate to the sunbelts. The demand for land is tremendous.

G: Are all the orchards gone from your town?

F: No. About two thousand acres are left. But I am afraid that our population, which is now about 52,000, will ultimately reach 100,000 or more. No groves will remain unless some are preserved in public ownership.

G: Why did you say "Redlands is about halfway between Los Angeles and Palm Springs?"

F: The rule for explaining anything is "advance from the known to the unknown." Although it is only a desert city, Palm Springs is famous. The rich, the powerful, and the celebrities make it so. Beginning with Harry Truman, every modern President has spent at least a few days relaxing there — usually on a golf course.

G: But you seem to be apologizing.

F: I am. It's rather absurd, from a geographer's point of view, to link Los Angeles, which is almost on the coast, with Palm Springs, which lies beyond a high mountain range on an arid desert. The only justification for this explanation is that it works.

G: I don't quite understand about this Santa Ana River. If it is a string which has attracted urban beads, why haven't I heard of it before?

F: If you speak of "a city on a river," I see a picture in my mind's eye. It is London, with Westminster Bridge across the Thames.

At the Orange Street Bridge in Redlands you seldom see much water except after a storm. The creek pours out of the mountains and is diverted for irrigation or sinks into the alluvial beds. We have a vast "lake," so to speak, underground. Water for irrigation and for domestic use is pumped from it.

G: Then how do these down-river cities you mentioned get any water?

F: The underground water percolates slowly down grade. When it comes to a dike — an impervious barrier made by an earthquake fault — it rises to the surface and flows. Again, it sinks and rises.

G: What is your term? Do you say that Redlands is situated in the "Upper Santa Ana Valley?"

F: Engineers may use that term in a technical report, but the common name is "the San Bernardino Valley." This may be modified to say: "Redlands is situated in the eastern San Bernardino Valley."

I don't care for the term "valley". Again, return to pictures in the mind's eye. Any Californian can conjure up an image of "Yosemite Valley" — deep, and with great walls of about equal height above the floor.

By the standard of Yosemite, our "valley" is a disappointment. It does have a north wall that rises to a ridge 6,000 feet high. But there is no corresponding elevation to the south. Also, the so-called "valley" just peters out to the west. Ask a native where it ends and he will only mutter.

G: Are there any better terms?

F: Not really. In the past decade or more "Inland Empire" has become popular. It is of synthetic origin and seeks to embrace Riverside, San Bernardino and Redlands. It attempts to give a name to a populous region rather than to a true geographical area.

G: Tell me about Los Angeles.

F: Redlands is on the plain that extends westward to L.A. and the sea. It is commonly said that we live in "the Los Angeles Basin" — a term that is frequently used in talk about air pollution. The basin traps smog.

Wherever people live in the world, they are likely to speak of "going to The City." In Redlands, "The City" means Los Angeles. It's the megalopolis of Southern California.

L.A. has great influence. All of the major television stations are there. Except for the networks, any news program will be Los Angeles centered. The *Los Angeles Times* is widely read in Redlands.

G: Two more topics and then we'd better get ready for our arrival. What did you say about an Air Base?

F: The destiny of a city can be beyond prediction. "Old Redlands" was the child of the navel orange. "New Redlands" is a by-product of national defense. Norton Air Force Base was established because it had become inevitable that the United States would be drawn into World War II. Hundreds of Redlands people were promptly employed there.

After the Japanese surrender it seemed the base would be closed within a few years. But the Cold War renewed the threat to America's survival.

Norton settled down as a permanent base for training crews of Air Force cargo planes.

With the coming of the Space Age, Norton also became a scientific and engineering headquarters for the development of long-range missiles.

In short, Redlands was transformed from a farming town into a military support city by forces in distant Europe and Asia.

G: Quite a transformation, I would say!

What was the "one more thing" you wanted to add?

F: About where Redlands is on the globe.

You British were so good at developing astronomy for navigation on the seas that geography describes the world with your country as the base line. The Greenwich Meridian divides the globe into halves—an orange cut in two. I have stood over the zero meridian line—a brass strip embedded in cement at the Greenwich Observatory—with one foot in the eastern hemisphere and one in the western hemisphere.

In the jet age, Redlands travelers most commonly experience the world in thirds, not halves. Today is typical. Our flight from London has taken us a third of the way around the world.

If a Redlander flies west, his trip to the Philippines will again take him a third of the way around the globe.

An academic view of geography? Yes. But it is useful information. It is the first step in understanding what time it is anywhere on earth.

When we took off from London today it was noon there and

The World in Thirds

4 A.M. here in California. As you well know, of course, a third of the world translates into a third of a 24-hour day, or eight hours.

I can't tell you how many people I used to help who were trying to telephone a son in the American Army in Japan but couldn't figure out what time it was there.

It has been a pleasure to fly with you Geoffrey, but I'm afraid I've done all of the talking. If we meet in the air again, it will be your turn. You can even the score. Happy landings!

Sun, Rain and Wind

THE ADVERTISING DEPARTMENT of the Union Pacific Railroad assigned a staff photographer to take a calendar picture that would say: "Come to California."

He knew where to look — Redlands, of course.

Quickly scouting the town, he found the view he wanted on the heights. Only one element in the scene was missing. The trees had been picked. Being a resourceful chap, he engaged a crew to pick oranges, leaving the stems long, and then to wire them into the foliage.

When printed, his colorful picture was a copy of the California image which many Easterners bear in mind while shoveling snow.

The sun was bright, the sky was cloudless blue. A good day for golf, it seemed to say.

Commanding the distance was the mighty pyramid of Mt. San Bernardino, the summit frosted with snow.

Framing his picture on either side were tall palm trees.

And in the foreground was that green-black foliage, decorated with ripe navel oranges. When picked they would be delicious to eat or to drink if squeezed into a glass.

There was much truth in his "California-here-I-come" photo. He had visualized our Mediterranean climate.

But it did not say why this is one of those rare places on Earth where the summers are hot and the winters are cool, and, periodically, rainy. Nor did it suggest the extremes of weather which have strongly influenced the destiny of our town. Both the summer heat and the winter rains are first explained by our latitude, by our north-south position on the globe.

The summer sun has plenty of wallop here because it is so

high in the sky. At the solstice in June the sun, standing over the Tropic of Cancer, shines more directly on Redlands than on a point on the Equator.

In winter most—but not all—of the powerful storms are brewed in the Gulf of Alaska. They come down over the Pacific Ocean, and, if the gate is open, reach us with rain and sometimes with snow. But more often than not they make landfall far to the north of us—Washington, Oregon and northern California—and migrate eastward. They bypass Redlands to the north.

We are near the end of the storm track. This you can verify by driving down Baja California for a hundred miles or so. There you find sparse vegetation that tells you the heavy rains from the north are not common visitors.

Of equal importance to latitude is our location on the North American continent. We are near the West Coast, being about 50 airline miles from the sea. On Monday a mass of maritime air may invade our valley. The day will be cool and overcast in the morning. On Tuesday the teeter-totter will tip the other way. The sky will be clear, the sun bright and the air warm.

We share our particular climate with only our neighbors in the Inland Empire, or as the weathermen call it, "The Intermediate Valley." Elsewhere in Southern California you will find about ten climate zones.

From San Diego to Santa Barbara the coastal climate is tempered by the ocean. The summer days are never as hot as they are inland nor are winter nights as cold. But the morning sun is frequently hidden by fog.

The farther inland you come, the less fog you encounter. That is why there are times when dozens of airliners cannot land at Los Angeles and are diverted to Ontario.

And the farther from the coast you come in the Great Valley of Southern California, the hotter a summer's day is likely to be.

Just to the north and east of us stand the San Bernardino Mountains. They have, of course, a much colder climate in winter and refreshing, cool weather in summer. In addition to wringing great quantities of rain and snow from the clouds for our benefit, they also wall us off from the deserts.

The elevation of the eastern San Bernardino Valley is another important factor in determining the climate. Most of the orange groves have been located between 1,200 and 2,000 feet above sea level. The maximum is about 2,400 feet. Above that, the winter nights are too cold.

Within the city, oranges on the heights seldom freeze on nights of light frost while on low ground some fruit may be nipped.

If wars are the landmarks in the general history of the world, the great freezes are the memorable events in the climatic history of Redlands. For the first half of the Twentieth Century, this was a one-industry town and that industry was citrus. We made our collective living by growing, packing, shipping and selling oranges and grapefruit. If the crops were damaged by frost, jobs were lost, growers borrowed from the banks, business was poor and there was no money to send Junior to college that year.

Although Redlanders began to plant orange groves in the 1880s, it took years to develop most of the available land. The optimists were able to persuade themselves that if this blessed spot was not entirely frost free, it was still economic to grow oranges here.

Then came the disastrous freeze of 1913. On the night of January 6–7, the temperature held at 22 degrees, or less, for eight hours. The minimum was 18.

So much fruit on the trees was frozen that pessimists concluded there was no future for citrus here. Legend has it that the population of Redlands shrank by 2,000 people. Whatever the actual figure may have been, a single case history will make the point.

A. E. Springborg had patiently built up a profitable jewelry business, but he decided that all of his effort had been in vain. He moved to Fresno.

The lesson of 1913 was that an orange grower on low ground had to provide frost protection for his fruit. He had to have

orchard heaters, oil storage, accu-
rate thermometers and a smudging crew. That wasn't enough. He
further needed weather forecasts
in great detail and specific to
Redlands.

The United States Weather
Bureau responded in 1921, estab-
lishing a Redlands district of the
new Fruit-Frost Service. A mete-

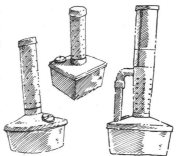

Smudge Pots

orologist would take up residence here each fall and stay almost
until spring. At 5 o'clock each afternoon he would telephone the
chief and they would finalize the forecast for the night.

Floyd D. Young was the father of the Fruit-Frost Service.
Each evening at 8 o'clock he would give his forecasts for all California and Arizona districts over the powerful radio station,
KFI. During freeze periods, hundreds of Redlanders would listen to him in their homes. They came to have tremendous
respect for him.

In time, "Fruit-Frost" evolved into the Agricultural Weather
Service, giving year-round forecasts for farmers. Redlanders
could be particularly comfortable with the chief, Ronald
Hamilton, a graduate of Redlands High School. He is of the
third Hamilton generation to live on and farm an East Highlands orange grove.

What those who fight frost learn is that a major freeze is not a
local event. If the minimum reaches 20 degrees here, it will also
be awfully cold in Central California and on the desert near
Indio. Why? Because a vast mass of Arctic air has swept down
from Canada, wide, deep and persistent.

High ground will be colder than low ground, at first. Heat
from the oil-burning smudge pots seems to go straight up. Fir-
ing must be long and heavy. Promptly on the next morning, the
pots must be refilled in readiness for the next night.

After World War II, many growers installed wind machines.
On a marginal night they mix the warmer air, above, with the

colder air near the ground and protect the fruit. If smudging becomes necessary, they help to spread the heat through the grove.

From about 1965 onward many orange groves were bull-dozed out, but many wind machines were left standing, lonely and flailing in the wind.

Many people coming to Redlands, however, have reacted much more to the summer heat than to the winter cold. Nearly half of the afternoons in July, August and September will bring maximum temperatures of 90 degrees or more. On the average, 15 of those will peak at 100 degrees or higher.

In earlier times everyone who could manage fled from Red-lands in summer—mostly to the beaches or the mountains. World War II ended that era.

The man-made environment began to change. Summer heat in this area is usually quite dry. That is favorable for evapo-rative coolers—the cheapest kind. They came into wide use in homes, stores and offices.

As refrigerated air cooling systems were improved, they were installed in more and more homes, offices and stores. Simulta-neously automobile air conditioning became common.

While the weather itself did not change, the prevailing atti-tude toward it surely did. People accepted summer. They adapted by wearing light clothes: commonly, shorts and short sleeves.

They bought or built homes with patios where they could bar-becue, eat and lounge. They installed private swimming pools by the hundreds.

The trade-off for a hot summer day is a balmy evening. It is pleasant to sit outdoors, under the stars. That is one reason the Tuesday and Friday programs of the Redlands Community Music Association attract so many to the Bowl. Oh, yes. While enjoying the concerts they don't have to swat mosquitoes.

Nor do they have to carry umbrellas. Only one concert out of a hundred will be cancelled, moved to the University Chapel or stopped in mid-performance by rain.

If a concert will be threatened in the evening, you will know it in the afternoon by looking to the mountains to the east. Cumulus clouds will build up, suggesting great heads of cauliflower. They may blacken in spots and thunderstorms will deluge the high country.

Those storms are created by tropical, moist air flowing up from the Gulf of Mexico or the Gulf of California. The origin of this weather was not understood until about 1930 and was not made graphic until earth satellites began to transmit photos of the Southwest and Mexico.

Satellites also show another type of summer rains that used to arrive without warning. They are the end product of hurricanes that are born in the tropical eastern Pacific Ocean and migrate northward. They tend to diminish in power and veer out to sea. But they occasionally turn toward the land and may hit such a tempting target as Acapulco.

A few will continue on a northward course until they are far up Baja California, veer east and cross the land. By then they have been downgraded in class to "tropical storms." Although bypassing Redlands to the south, they can bring tremendous downpours to the city.

If you live here for some years, you will come to remember them by their hurricane names. For example: "Kathleen. September 10 and 11, 1976."

The City of Redlands was only three years old when it was baptized by a "cloudburst." On August 11, 1891, water poured down the slope of the town, and State Street became a river at flood tide. Redlanders got the message. They voted bonds to build a system of flood ditches.

Because these sudden floods come so infrequently, people who live near the channels have no awareness of the danger they can present. Thus, no one pays attention to children who play in them. Two boys were swept from near Palm Avenue to town and, somehow, survived. One little girl, playing near Cypress and Buena Vista, was caught, drowned and carried beyond Brookside Avenue.

Although the Redevelopment Agency financed a large box culvert in 1986 to carry the outflow of Reservoir Canyon to the underground Zanja in town, a major threat remains at this writing. Collecting thunderstorm waters from as far east as the Crafton Hills, the Zanja can send a river down Redlands Boulevard. The Council recognized this possibility by requiring new buildings along that thoroughfare to be built on raised pads. Home Savings and Loan at Orange Street was the first one built under the ordinance.

While the brief summer rains can be memorable, most of our annual precipitation comes in winter—especially December, January, February and March. Our typical storm originates in the Gulf of Alaska and travels down to our latitude. With luck we will get an inch or two of rain and a new blanket of snow on the mountains. Without luck, the disturbance will peter out. As one meteorologist phrased it: "This is a land of dying storms."

Winter can also bring storms up from the waters between Southern California and Hawaii. In local history March 2, 1938, is a red letter date because of the warm front rain that brought the most damaging flood of the century. Three inches of rain fell in Redlands in less than 24 hours.

Engineers scoff at the popular belief that the flood was greatly intensified by rain falling on the snowy mountains. One noted hydrologist put it this way: "The amount of melt-water produced by rain is ordinarily trivial."

The Noah's-flood class storms produce so much precipitation that they confuse popular thinking about the average annual rainfall. This figure ranges from approximately 14 to 15 inches, depending upon the years included in the calculation. (The most recent figure, for 98 years, is 14.18 inches.)

Laurence S. Morrison, a native of Redlands, analyzed the matter in great detail in 1964 and wrote me a 16-page letter from his home in West Hartford, Connecticut. His point was that people assume it is normal to have a season of average rainfall. On the contrary, the seasonal totals vary so widely that an average year is rare.

Reviewing the record from 1892 to 1954, he found the magic average, 15 inches, for only one season. In a normal year the total will deviate from that benchmark to give a range from 9.4 to 19.2 inches. By this way of reckoning, there were 11 dry years, 41 normal years and 11 wet years in the 63-year period.

In 1951 E. D. Higgenbotham, orange grower, made a common-sense observation about precipitation. He classified storms into two types: "Soaking — storms which add both to surface and underground reserves. Dusters — storms of only minor value to surface supply of moisture; or of no value, like .10, .20, and .30 of an inch and far apart."

The distinction was startling for 1950–1951: total, 10.77, soakers, 1.64, dusters, 9.13.

In dry seasons the fancies of water-minded people turn to the possibilities — some how, some way — of increasing the rainfall. In 1915–16 there had been the legendary "Hatfield, the Rainmaker." Like Merlin the Magician, he went about his secret incantations. Just then a tremendous storm was already sweeping in over all of Southern California. A dam near San Diego washed out.

Soon after World War II, laboratory evidence suggested that clouds could be made more productive if they were artificially seeded. This idea came into sudden vogue here in 1947 when the Bear Valley Mutual Water Company, headquartered in Redlands, engaged a pilot to scatter dry ice pellets by plane on clouds hanging over Big Bear Lake. That opened an era of experimentation involving many agencies that did not fizzle out until 1981.

No one could prove to the satisfaction of those who were paying the bills that cloud seeding actually increased the natural precipitation. On top of that it became obvious that rain is most wanted in a dry spell but there is no way to create clouds to "milk" in an all-blue sky.

Natural rains often bring thunder and lightning — especially after winter cold front passages and during tropical-bred summer storms. The bolts strike transformers and electric wires, knocking out circuits and giving the Southern California Edison crews a workout. In 1987 lightning shattered a large deodar tree at the home of Waldo Burroughs.

House fires of this origin are so rare that you can't find a single lightning rod unless you know where to look. In 1927 Dr. Walter Power built a Spanish-style house which stands on a knoll just north across the golf course from the country club. He installed a mighty lightning rod worthy of a Jovian thunderbolt.

If lightning is kind to Redlands, cruel winds are the trade-off. Most frequently they are the notorious Santa Anas. In popular thinking, any strong, dry wind from the north is a Santa Ana. A fierce one will topple hundreds of ornamental trees, taking particular aim on aged giants. If a fire starts in the front country to the north, airborne embers will be carried ahead, much as if an incendiary raid were being conducted by enemy bombers. At night the mountains seem to be erupting lava.

Meterologists know, however, that there is a second type which strikes the valley soon after the passage of a cold front. For example, on January 16, 1949, the wind gusted to 63 miles-per-hour at Norton AFB. On the north-facing rows of Redlands orchards, oranges were whipped, scarred, punctured and plucked.

Fortunately, Redlands is situated far enough from the common path of the wind out of Cajon Pass to escape ordinary blows. This can be appreciated if you drive west from Redlands on the freeway and find that you are crossing through a stream of Santa Ana about 5 to 10 miles wide.

Preceding the 1949 blow, orange growers had fought a major freeze. At least some snow had fallen on the golf course on five consecutive days.

It is common that when snow falls, the Redlands heights will be white and the low ground will not. Because the U.S. Weather Service station is situated at a low elevation, the record does not give a satisfactory picture of the frequency, or infrequency, of "back East weather" in our town.

In concluding this chapter on climate and weather, I should

explain that I have not forgotten fall and spring. They are transitional periods in Redlands, lacking the bold personality of winter and summer.

They have an exasperating way of advancing and retreating. In 1985 we had high-ground snow on November 12 and an 80-degree maximum shortly before Christmas. It can be hot for a few days in March with frost on roof tops in early April.

The more dependable expressions of the seasons are given by some of our colorful plants and trees. In the fall the crape myrtle leaves turn to copper. The showy liquidambars dress in autumn hues. In May the jacarandas first lift their purple blossoms for the admiration of passers-by, and then they shower the ground with them. The oleanders, which seem to grow everywhere, announce with red, pink and white flowers that "summer is icumen in." You just have to get the hang of our seasons to enjoy the changes they bring.

I Lift My Eyes to the Mountains

GO WHERE YOU WILL within Redlands in fair weather, the mountains are always in sight. From almost cradle to grave, this is so.

When taken from the maternity ward at the hospital, the newborn baby is in the arms of a mother who may well see Mt. San Bernardino before she steps into a waiting automobile.

MT. SAN BERNARDINO

Mt. San Bernardino, Mt. San Gorgonio (Grayback)

When the mourners are gathered by the grave at Hillside Memorial Park and the minister reads: "I lift mine eyes unto the hills," the mountains are there to be seen.

From them Redlanders gather strength when it is most needed. It may be after a day when things have gone wrong. She is upset. She takes a walk. The high mountains, silent and present as always are catching the late rays of the sun. Although the sun sets and the city is in shadow, the peaks continue to glow.

She is calmed.

Yet, Redlanders seldom speak to one another about the glories of the three ranges that are within their sight. Indeed, many of them do not even know which is Mt. San Bernardino (10,691 ft.) and which is the highest of them all, Mt. San Gor-

MT. SAN GORGONIO
(Grayback)

gonio (11,499 ft.). They may ask occasionally. They listen to the answer for a moment, and then they forget.

This chapter, then, is about the visible mountains.

Of the three ranges, the San Jacinto is the least easily seen. It is situated to the southeast and the land of Redlands slopes upward in that direction. If the topography is not in your way, our many ornamental trees may well be.

But there is one place in Redlands where Mt. San Jacinto (10,804 ft.) is seen straight ahead, unobstructed, and in the very center of your view. That is when you are driving on the freeway, eastbound, and have passed through the center of town. The road now swings to your right and is aimed precisely at the distant mountain. It is as if the designers of the route had wanted to entice you onward, to lead you closer and closer.

Indeed, if you really want to see San Jacinto, you must continue onward through the San Gorgonio Pass. At Whitewater the front of the mountain rises with steepness worthy of the Sierra Nevada. The snow in the gullies will make streamers down the face until summer.

Continuing by car until you enter Palm Springs, a road on your right leads to the base of the Mt. San Jacinto Tramway. From there you can ride in a large car, suspended from a cable, to the shoulder of the mountain at Desert View. If you are in condition for hiking, the summit can be reached in three hours or less. — No !

It is a peculiarity of our mountain ranges that they seem to belong to those who live nearest to them. San Jacinto is in Riverside County and, therefore, not "ours." When a Redlander goes there, his destination will most likely be the charming village of Idyllwild.

If San Jacinto can seem to play "hide and seek" with Redlanders, the San Gabriel Range is never out of sight from any location within the city. The most impressive view is from the Smiley Heights tract. Looking to the northwest the foreground rapidly slopes away to the broad floor of the valley. Beyond, the mountains rise abruptly. They extend westward from the Cajon

Pass gap as far as the eye can see.

In summer, the sun will set over the range, causing the mass to stand in silhouette with sharply defined ridge lines. In winter the hump of Mt. Baldy, white with snow, will rise a bit above a ridge which tries to hide it, but fails.

As with the San Jacinto Range, the view of the San Gabriel becomes far more dramatic as you see it closer at hand. When you approach Ontario Airport on Interstate 10, the mountain wall makes a sheer rise to Cucamonga Peak (8,859 ft.).

But the truly magnificent view of Baldy is seen in winter while driving on Interstate 10 from Montclair to Claremont. The lower mountains open up and the peak then commands the range. The broad, long, snow slope is dazzling.

The Spanish-Californians called the range "Sierra Madre" or "mother mountains." I much prefer that name and blame Josiah Dwight Whitney for renaming it. He did so because so much of its waters flow into the San Gabriel River. Whitney, of course, was the surveyor for whom the highest peak in the Sierra Nevada is named.

There is also a problem about the name of the 10,064-foot peak, the highest summit of the range. The official designation is "Mt. San Antonio." But scarcely anyone calls it that. They may say "Old Baldy," or "Mt. Baldy" or just plain "Baldy."

Whatever your preference, you can impress people with your knowledge by telling them that the peak is the one point on the San Bernardino/Los Angeles County line that you can see from Redlands.

Although you need a clear morning and a telescope to see it, Mt. Wilson (5,710 ft.) can be picked out on the most distant foot of the San Gabriel range. The white domes of the astronomical observatory will identify the peak for you. As you continue to look you will probably be able to see several tall masts on the skyline.

Mt. Wilson is the television mountain for nearly everyone living in the Los Angeles basin. There is a direct line of sight to the homes of millions of people, including those in Redlands. Many

Los Angeles radio stations also transmit from the same peak.

In the history of science Mt. Baldy and Mt. Wilson are forever linked. On those two summits the great physicist, Albert A. Michelson, located the apparatus with which he measured the speed of light in 1926. His calculation was the best that had ever been made — 186,335 miles per second.

As San Jacinto belongs to Riverside County, the San Gabriel range gives no rise to possessive feelings among Redlanders. If they go there at all, it is most likely that they will be skiing at Wrightwood or its neighbor, Big Pine.

Little known to Redlanders is the Angeles Crest road, the most purely scenic highway in the three ranges. Mile after mile it winds along the slopes, about as high in elevation as the topography allows. There is one magnificent view across the San Gabriel River canyon to the back side of Baldy. More often, however, the view is north to the Mojave Desert. It's 74 miles from the Cajon Pass freeway to La Cañada, near Pasadena, at the west end of the road. And then you still have to drive more than an hour to get back to Redlands.

Although the San Bernardino range extends from Cajon Pass to the San Gorgonio Pass, it is not a single massif as seen from Redlands. Rather, we see a long, straight wall to the north. To the east are the mighty peaks. Dominating the range is the great pyramid of Mt. San Bernardino. Farther east, San Gorgonio raises its bare summit — the highest point in all of Southern California.

As Redlanders see it, the top of the north wall is approximately 30 miles long. At night the lights of houses show that the western half is well populated. The darkness to the east tells you of the absence of man.

With a flair for names, the mountain boosters of early times called the road along the ridge "The Rim of the World." Some folks still do. Two state highways lead up to it from the valley. The Waterman Canyon Grade is approached from San Bernardino. The City Creek Grade starts at Highland, almost straight across the Santa Ana Wash from Redlands.

Strangely, two mountains with summits lower than the Rim of the World stand forward from it. If fog curtains off the background, they seem to be the only mountains.

The more easterly of the presidential twins, Mt. Harrison (4,743 ft.), is easily identified by its greater elevation and by its flat top. You have probably seen it in photographs taken from the steps of the University Administration Building. If so, the mountain appeared to be about on a level with the steeple of the majestic chapel.

Mt. Harrison

Harrison's presidential companion, Mt. McKinley (3,795 ft.), stands just to the west and across City Creek Canyon. The tiny San Manuel Indian Reservation, near Patton, nestles at the base.

Chaparral covers the steep slopes of the front country. This dense, tough brush grows in the spring when the roots are wet and the radiation from the sun is intense. During the fierce heat of summer it begins to dry out and by fall is vulnerable to wild fires. Furthermore, litter accumulates on the ground, adding to the tinder.

In the late nineteenth century, sawmills started forest fires which burned, uncontrolled. Alarmed by the damage to their watershed, farmers and orange growers headed for Washington, D.C. There they succeeded in getting a presidential proclamation to establish a preserve which evolved to become San Bernardino National Forest. Today, the rangers have a far-flung organization for preventing fires and fighting them when they do break out.

The fires tend to erase some landmarks. One of them is the natural Arrowhead, at the base of the mountains just north of San Bernardino. When the brush recovers somewhat, the symbol shows fairly well if you are near it. But it is always difficult to see from Redlands because the angle is not face-on, and the distance is great. If you want to hunt for it with binoculars, Smiley Heights is the best location because of its westerliness in Redlands and its elevation.

The False Arrowhead

Confusing to many people is what might be called the "False Arrowhead." This is a bare, whitish gulch, gouged in a head of Fredalba Creek just below Running Springs. It is almost due north of Redlands and at high elevation instead of at the mountain base.

You will have no uncertainty, however, about the large block "R" about a mile farther east. This is the emblem of the University of Redlands. In 1913 a band of enthusiastic students whacked it out of the brush. In following years male members of the freshman class were required to go up once a year and clean it. On special occasions the letter would be lighted with red railroad flares, a spectacular sight.

You may have wondered about the road seen below the "R" starting at the base of the mountains and climbing in a zigzag. That is the Alder Creek truck trail, built by the Forest Service to give fire-fighting access to the middle elevation of the front country.

Three miles to the east, Keller Peak (7,882 ft.) rises as the highest point. In summer and fall an observer is stationed in the fire lookout. That is one of the three towers visible from Redlands. The others are Strawberry Peak (6,153 ft.) to the north, and Morton Peak (4,624 ft.) to the east.

Just east of Keller is Slide Peak (7,779 ft.), the highest point in

KELLER PEAK

Keller Peak

the Snow Valley ski-lift complex.

Scan the skyline eastward and you first see the Bear Creek gap. From there the watershed divide between Bear Valley and the Santa Ana Canyon extends to Sugar Loaf.

All of the long ridge to the north, which I have described, is usually seen by Redlanders without emotion. It is when they turn their attention eastward to Mt. San Bernardino and San Gorgonio that they are stirred.

Why? Because no mark of man is visible on the range. No aerial tramway ascends the face of San Bernardino. No restaurant perches on the apex of the pyramid.

Indeed, it is hard to imagine that anyone has ever tried to climb the forbidding face of the mountain.

Protected from change by the National Wilderness Act, Mt. San Bernardino will always stand as a visible refuge from the tensions of city life.

The great mountain looks today as it did before the white man came to the valley. It will look the same as long as there is a city called Redlands.

We gaze with awe upon the unspoiled, eternal mountain.

Living in Earthquake Country

TOURISTS BY THE THOUSANDS flocked to Redlands in the early years to view the magnificent scenery. They were driven over Smiley Heights and saw the land sloping down to the broad valley and then rising abruptly to the ridges and peaks of the San Bernardino Mountains.

Few of them understood that these grand land forms are accompanied by a feature they could not see—faults. These fractures in the crust of the Earth are a byproduct of the forces that have shaped our fascinating landscape.

If they stayed in town for any length of time, they would inevitably have a new experience for which they were not mentally prepared.

This is earthquake country.

At 11:29 P.M. on February 23, 1892, windows rattled. Downtown, at the Baker House, a frightened man jumped from a window to a lower roof. A merchant, apparently working late, rushed out with a shotgun hollering that someone was trying to rob him. Hotel guests dashed outdoors in their nightclothes.

Their reaction was normal. Excitement and confusion accompany any lively quake. Charles Darwin, father of Evolution, explained why after an experience in Chile in 1835: "A bad earthquake at once destroys our oldest association; the Earth, the very emblem of solidity, has moved beneath our feet like thin crust over fluid."

The more you know about earthquakes, however, the more you can keep your head. Indeed, you may even learn to enjoy them. This chapter may help you become a connoisseur of our California specialty.

Redlands is situated between two faults—the San Andreas

and the San Jacinto. A set of minor faults underlies the town.

The approximate location of the San Andreas is simple to see. It is the line where the mountains rise abruptly from the floor of the valley. That is, it extends along the northern edge of San Bernardino, Del Rosa, Highland and East Highlands.

Although this is the most famous of all California faults there is only one official sign on it. That is at La Cienega winery which is not far from Hollister but hundreds of miles from Redlands.

For a time there was as second one, erected by the U.S. Forest Service. When driving from Redlands and Mentone on State Route 38 you would see it on your left, just before reaching the Edison power house at the mouth of Mill Creek Canyon. Vandals swiped it.

Dr. Stephen Dana, University of Redlands geologist at the time, was philosophical. He said it had been in the wrong place. The fault goes right under the Mill Creek ranger station, en route to Oak Glen and Pine Bench.

A more northerly branch of the San Andreas extends into the mountains where it has created a straight, long valley with steep sides. Redlanders can thank the fault system for most of Mill Creek Canyon, a place of commanding beauty, a cool refuge from our warm valley, and a major source of irrigation and domestic water.

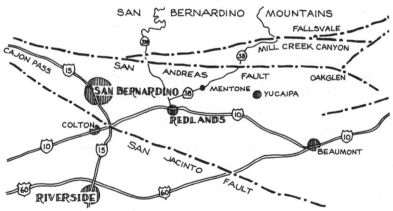

Major Faults (adapted from Iacopi's Earthquake Country*)*

It is the fault that sheers the north wall above Fallsvale. Left in a hanging valley, Falls Creek plunges over the precipice. Alas, many young men have been lured to those treacherous cliffs and died.

Because the San Andreas is the celebrity fault of California, it is frequently talked and written about. Unless you pay attention, you may get the notion that it moves somewhat like a freight train. If the locomotive goes forward, so must the caboose. Not so with the fault.

In the twentieth century, the behavior of the fault has varied in segments. Far to the north the massive quake of 1906 severely damaged buildings from Santa Rosa to San Francisco and Palo Alto. Farther south, at Hollister, the fault continually creeps. Yet, along the segment near Redlands there is no evidence of either creep or displacement in modern times.

The fashionable theory holds that a mighty strain is building up. Sooner or later we will experience a violent quake. If this is true — and it may not be — the jolt could come today or not for a couple of hundred years.

Coming down from the Cajon Pass, the San Jacinto fault slices through San Bernardino — specifically, through the campus of Valley College. Continuing across the valley it passes under the northeast quadrant of the Octopus, the sprawling freeway interchange south of San Bernardino and east of Colton. Then it heads for the east side of Reche Canyon and bends across the upper slopes of the hills on the far side of San Timoteo Canyon.

If you stand on Sunset Drive near the cemetery and look south across the canyon, you will see a eucalyptus plantation, high on the far hills. The San Jacinto passes just below the square of dark green trees on its way to the town of San Jacinto, near Hemet.

Judging by experience — not by theory — it is the San Jacinto, rather than the San Andreas, which should worry us. Twice within 19 years it was vengeful. In 1899 it gave San Jacinto a terrible Christmas present — an earthquake that knocked down brick and adobe buildings and killed six Indians. On April 21,

1918, it played an encore. No one died, but San Jacinto was left in shambles.

The 1918 shock was heavy in Redlands.

Three of our strongest earthquakes centered in the ground beneath Reche Canyon in an area about four miles southwest of Redlands. That's on the San Jacinto, the fault to watch.

The minor faults which underlie Redlands are a quite different story.

A fault only causes an earthquake when it moves. We have no evidence that local fractures have even so much as rattled our windows. But the fact is we don't know what their meaning is for the long term. They could remain as harmless as a kitten forever. Yet, it is possible they could cause trouble. Look to the San Fernando fault. It was thought to be inactive but in 1971 inflicted great loss of life and property in San Fernando and Sylmar.

The reason we know so little about these minor faults is that geologists "hunt where the ducks are." That is, they study the most threatening faults, especially the San Andreas. There appear to be no ducks in Redlands. So no thorough investigation, utilizing advanced but expensive technology, has ever been undertaken.

Two studies, though, were illuminating.

Geologists of the U.S. Geological Survey published a report in 1972 on an intensive study they made here. They were not concerned with faults as the source of potential earthquakes. They were concentrating on them as barriers to the underflow of ground water, the object of their research.

Their map shows various ground-water basins and sub-basins which underlie the Redlands Heights. The primary boundaries include the Redlands Fault, the Crafton Fault, the Redlands Heights Fault, and the Banning Fault.

What this means to a layman is that we have areas where water can be pumped on intermediate and high ground because there are faults to retain it in basins.

Back in 1913 the founders of our city water system recognized this when they drilled a set of wells in what is now Ford Park. Situated just above a fault, and at the mouth of Reservoir Canyon, this basin has served Redlands for generations.

On the other hand, the pursuit of these locations can be dismaying and costly. The Redlands Country Club is not far from a well located close to the Redlands Heights Fault, just off upper Ford Street. If good water was found there, why not on the club property? Thousands of dollars could be saved by pumping for the golf course. As it turned out, thousands were expended in a fruitless hunt for ground water.

The second study was a direct investigation of the location of our faults. Diana Dana conducted it in 1982-83 as an honors project at the University of Redlands.

Although she found that she occasionally attracted more attention than a sideshow, she persisted in going up and down selected streets. She would stop to take extremely careful readings with an instrument that detects very small differences in the force of gravity. It can delineate geological structures far below the surface.

If you had her map in hand, you could draw a line straight south from Colton and Orange to Hillside Memorial Park. It would cross three main faults and four branches of the Crafton Fault. In general, they would intersect your line at right angles, that is, east and west. None are oriented north-south.

To put it more simply — if you live in Redlands your home is within half-a-mile, at most, of a fault. It is not unlikely that you live right on one.

If we have seven faults, why can't you see even one? Because they are concealed beneath the alluvium on which Our Town stands. Only one surface expression of a fracture survived the grading and scraping of the ground for homes, streets and groves.

On the University of Redlands campus it is called "Ad (Administration) Hill." That's the "acropolis" on which the Administration Building stands.

A half mile to the west, the uplift rises steeply from Colton

Avenue to the higher street, The Terrace.

In geological time, Diana found, that faulting is part of the process by which the Redlands Heights have been elevated from the valley floor.

If viewing The Terrace puts you in an exploratory mood, you may wish to search for the San Andreas Fault on the far side of our valley. Then turn to Robert Iacopi's excellent Sunset Book: *Earthquake Country — How, Why and Where Earthquakes Strike in California.* His maps and photographs of "The San Bernardino Area" are easy to follow.

I find that early local history about earthquakes is based largely on newspaper accounts. Often the writers were more inclined toward humor than toward careful and thorough fact-finding. Their accounts must be taken with a grain of salt.

Since 1918, our quakes have been measured by seismograph, so the data is scientific and reliable.

Imperfect though the early record may be, one cardinal fact stands out: Redlands has never experienced a major earthquake. We have never known one that would hold a candle to San Francisco, 1906.

We have had about four medium earthquakes. All the rest have been inconsequential.

You must look to the important earthquakes that have centered elsewhere for influence on Redlands.

Foremost in this set of seismic events was the Long Beach disaster of 1933. Everyone was horrified by the collapse of school buildings in that city. If the event had come when the students were in them—instead of at 5:54 P.M. — scores of boys and girls would have been killed. Public clamor was loud.

Within two months our Legislature wrote and passed the Field Act. New school buildings would have to meet stringent engineering standards to make them as earthquake resistant as possible.

Constructed under this new code, the Girls' Gymnasium at Redlands High School contained so much steel that Gordon Donald, a veteran contractor, scratched his head in wonderment.

However, it was not the Field Act that stimulated new school construction in the late 1930s but the need to replace obsolete buildings. Down came the two-story, voluminous McKinley Elementary School to be replaced by a low, long building of radical design. The Lincoln Elementary School (now Orangewood High) on Texas Street followed in the same style.

Although municipal governments were not required to act, the City of Redlands did pay attention to its own buildings. Inspecting the A. K. Smiley Public Library in 1936, City Engineer George Hinckley found that the tower had not been designed to resist the horizontal forces that had been so destructive in Long Beach. The Council awarded a contract to Bert Taylor to remove the top floor. When the job was finished, the picturesque roof which had given the building so much style, was gone. The truncated base looked then, and looks now, as if its top had been sawed off.

In the next decade, public attention shifted from local affairs to one overriding concern—World War II. It was not until the great Tehachapi temblor of 1952 that Redlands officials became earthquake minded again.

Original Library Tower   *Truncated Library Tower*

Our City Building Inspector, Ray Phelps, went up to Tehachapi and was strongly impressed by something he saw that per-
tained to Redlands. The parapets — the false fronts raised above
the roof line — of old brick business buildings had toppled forward onto the sidewalks.

Fearing that Redlands shoppers would be "bombed" by cas-
cading bricks, Phelps asked the City Council to adopt an ordinance that would require the removal of dangerous parapets.
The Council demurred.

That was not the end of the matter. Whenever the owner of a
Downtown building applied for a permit to alter a facade,
Phelps insisted on proper engineering for the new parapet. The
cumulative result of his efforts, over a period of years, was
impressive.

In the next decade, the Sixties, the School Board was stirred
to action by a peculiar twist of events. The Legislature re-codi-
fied the Law of Torts. When the Board's counsel read it under a
magnifying glass, so to speak, he was alarmed. Under his inter-
pretation, each Trustee would be personally liable for the injury
or death of students in a collapsing school building unless he had
taken vigorous action to prevent the catastrophe.

There was no other course open to the Board. A structural
engineer was hired to make a building-by-building survey. The
citizenry was incredulous of his report.

The reinforced concrete buildings of the 1920s that looked as
solid as the Rock of Gibraltar to the populace, looked like death
traps to him. He explained that roofs, walls and foundations
should have been bonded together, forming sturdy boxes.
Instead, he found roof trusses resting atop walls, held in place
only by the vertical force of gravity. If the walls moved sideways
the roofs would cave in, he said.

The citizens grudgingly consented to the replacement of
Kingsbury, Franklin, and the former Redlands Junior High.

Clock Auditorium at the high school was salvaged by beefing
it up. Such irony! Clock happens to be our homeliest building
because the original plans for a magnificent structure proved to

be too costly. The plan was stripped of all amenities and beauty — inside and out — giving us an ugly duckling.

To this day there are hundreds of Redlanders who believe that if a building was made of concrete it was safe. In their opinions the tearing down of 1920s structures was nonsense.

While school officials were replacing hazardous buildings, water officials were working on a puzzle of their own.

Water coming down from northern California emerges from a tunnel near California State University, San Bernardino. To distribute it for the use of San Bernardino, Highland, Redlands and Yucaipa, a big pipeline would have to be laid along the foot of the mountains. It just so happens that Nature put the San Andreas Fault on the optimum line for the pipe.

The first decision was to locate the transmission line parallel to the fault but keeping a respectful distance from it. Still, the pipe had to cross the fault at some point. How should that be done?

District Engineer Louis Fletcher decided that it was futile to try to build an unbreakable section across the hazard zone. Rather, the sensible course was to design the pipe so that it could be quickly repaired, using standard sections.

When "The Big One" comes, the Muni pipe should break just below the Devil Canyon Power House, releasing a brief, harmless flood into the spreading grounds below.

Muni had no more than made up its mind about the transmission line when earthquake hazards became a renewed, statewide concern. On February 9, 1971, a killer earthquake struck the San Fernando area. Sixty-four people died. Hospital buildings — old and new — failed.

As the Long Beach earthquake had provoked the Legislature to adopt the Field Act, the San Fernando disaster precipitated the Alquist-Priolo Act. State authorities would designate geological hazard zones. No one could build on a site within one unless the ground was studied and approved by a geologist.

Because the State Geologist did not classify Redlands as a place within a hazard zone, Alquist-Priolo has had no effect here. It is in north San Bernardino, on the San Andreas, that developers have provided full employment for certified geologists.

Caltrans, however, needed no prodding from the Legislature to apply the lessons of San Fernando.

Directly bearing on Redlands was dramatic evidence that bridges carrying freeways over local streets can fail. If a deck slides back-and-forth far enough, one end will no longer rest on an abutment. It will fall.

Caltrans adopted a program to correct this condition wherever it existed on the state system. In Redlands the bridges which carry I-10 over our streets were found to be satisfactory. However, restrainers were applied to the long bridge over I-10 on the "Tennessee Street Freeway," Route 30.

Restrainers were also applied to the bridges of the Octopus, the sprawling interchange between Redlands and Colton.

The San Fernando earthquake having wrecked the Veterans Hospital, a new one was needed and in a safer location. The Administration selected a site in Loma Linda. An uproar followed. What folly to replace one hospital with another on a second dangerous fault! That's what critics said.

The Administration hired a big league consulting firm to investigate the site. A deep trench was dug diagonally across the property and shored up. Geologists went down in it and inch-by-inch searched for the signature of a fault. They did not find one. Nor did test drilling bring up any telltale material. Construction proceeded. The hospital was named for the late Congressman Jerry Pettis who had convinced the Veterans Administration that Loma Linda was the right place.

In the years following the San Fernando disaster, the State Seismic Safety Commission had its work cut out for it. Robert Rigney of Redlands was eventually elected chairman. As an executive of San Bernardino County government he was responsible for a county building at Rancho Cucamonga that allows the earth to move with minimal shaking of the structure.

County Supervisor Barbara Riordan of Redlands later

became a member of the Seismic Commission.

Reverberations from San Fernando proved long lasting. At Lake Arrowhead the state required costly replacement of the original earthfill dam. At Bear Valley a new dam in place of the concrete one built in 1911 is going to be built, sooner or later.

In Redlands the quaint Phinney Building of 1892 on Orange Street has been saved by installing a steel frame. This is the home of the finest restaurant Our Town has ever had—Joe Greensleeves.

Engineers are proceeding with a similar framing project for the A. K. Smiley Public Library.

You might suppose that with all this earthquake conscious-ness we would have a seismograph in Redlands. We don't—not a scientific one. We depend on the seismographic laboratory of Caltech, in Pasadena, for data.

Until an instrument is installed here—perhaps at the County Museum—we will have to get along with human detectors. They work on the second floor of the bank building at the corner of Citrus and Orange. Their chairs vibrate beneath them when-ever the earth moves a smidgin. Why this is the most sensitive spot in town is uncertain. Perhaps the steel floor of the corridor amplifies the quaking.

When the "Big One" comes, how will Redlands fare?

Centering somewhere in our region this oft-predicted earth-quake will cause strong ground shaking for miles around. We share this risk with all who live in earthquake country.

There will be much excitement. Weak structures will be dam-aged. Emergency services will probably be necessary.

However, we do not live in an unfavorable location in earth-quake country.

Redlands does not overlie a major fault such as the San Andreas or the San Jacinto.

We do not have a water table which is so near the surface as to cause failure of the overlying ground.

Our soil is not poor, creating a hazard that displacement would cause many breaks in gas, sewer and water lines.

Rather, the red soil on which so much of Redlands stands is old alluvium which is fairly well consolidated and compact. We have built on a good geological foundation. That is much in our favor.

With a Passion for Trees

In Our Town we have more trees than people.

Beautifying the streets and boulevards are nearly 30,000 crapes, palms, oaks and others. In addition there are thousands of trees in parks, along the freeway, and on private property.

Look at the site of nearly every single-family home and you will see at least one tree. The owner of even the smallest lot will usually place a shade-giving specimen at the back, if not in front.

This passion for trees began a century ago. And no wonder. The flat, the slope and the heights were barren when settlement began. There may have been a few clumps of California live oaks, some cottonwoods around a spring, and elderberries here and there. The only long line of leafy trees marked the course of the Zanja.

Read letters written by those who lived in the first houses in the Redlands Colony and it's a good bet you'll encounter a remark about the strong winds.

If the common wisdom does have a basis in fact, we have less violent winds today than in, say, 1882, because of our abundant trees.

Beauty, though, was what the early settlers sought. Redlands Patron Saints, Albert and Alfred Smiley, preached the gospel that landscaping is not only good aesthetics. It is also good business. A quality town tends to attract quality people.

E. G. Judson, co-founder and first mayor of Redlands, was also a "missionary." From his own modest nursery he would give trees to citizens who would plant them properly and care for them.

Thanks to the zeal of our forefathers, we now have thousands of California fan palms that are nearly a century old. You will find them on many streets, but Cajon is the king of them all.

From City Hall, drive up this commanding boulevard and for over a mile you are walled in by these tall, stout trunks. Take a tally and your total will go over 200.

When John Hiatt, a horticulture major from Cal Poly, Pomona, took a census of Redlands street trees in 1984, he found 3,489 of this variety. They are visually dominant, overwhelming the smaller but more numerous (6,228) crape myrtles.

If you stand where you look over the general mass of our trees, however, you will see another palm that profiles against the mountains or the sky. This is the first cousin of the California fan palm—the Mexican fan palm. The trunk is like a pole. In high wind it becomes flexible and bends as if it were a coconut palm.

To distinguish these trees, go to the Post Office on Brookside Avenue. Growing along the curb are the Mexican fan palms. You will have to bend your neck to look all the way up the thin trunk to the fronds. This variety extends westward on the south side of Brookside.

Just across the way are the California fan palms—not so slim and not quite so tall. They, too, extend westward but on the north curb line.

In the divider you will notice two islands, in a line, each with cocos plumosa. That was the standard tree of the business dis-

Cocos Plumosa
Palm

California
Fan Palm

Mexican
Fan Palm

trict streets at one time, but the merchants tired of these smaller palms. Many were removed. Nonetheless, Hiatt found that this is the sixth most common street tree (846) in Redlands. On some residence district thoroughfares they are the only variety for half a mile.

Landscaping on Brookside from just west of the Post Office to beyond San Mateo represents the beau ideal of Judson and Brown.

Riverside was developed about a decade before Redlands, and it was there our founders went for inspiration and practical guidance. They were so taken by the plan of divided boulevards with planting in the median and on the outer curbs that they tried to follow suit. Their ambitions were bigger than their pocketbooks. Only Brookside resembles Riverside's Magnolia Avenue.

While the palms along Brookside are about as old as the street, the oaks in the median are not. The original planting was of peppers. Redlanders loved these evergreens for their grace — a spreading tree with light green foliage that weeps as low to the ground as you will allow. Small red berries hang in clusters.

Alas, the pepper is not a long-lived tree. In time, disease hollows out the wood. The branches, if long, may snap off in a high wind and fall. Those who love peppers "died hard" about their removal by the city. Remaining specimens are so severely pruned that they are without grace.

The oaks which replaced them on Brookside are shaping up well and should last well into the next century.

You might suppose that the coast live oak, because it is native to nearby Live Oak Canyon, would be the best for Redlands. Not so. They tend to be too big for the ground available between a curb and a sidewalk. In maturity they may have grandeur, giving distinction to such streets as upper Buena Vista. But then root fungus starts to take its toll. One is removed here and there. Then the planting begins to look ragged.

Learning from experience, the city switched to the better oak for Redlands — the holly oak. This well-formed evergreen with dense foliage has become the third most common street tree (2,228).

A century of experience has taught us that some of the original favorites were mistakes and never should have been planted.

In their enthusiasm for Australia's gift to California, the eucalyptus, our grandfathers failed to exclude species that reach for the clouds. When such a giant crashes down in a Santa Ana wind, it smashes whatever is in the way — orange trees, stone walls, barns.

Hundreds of eucalyptus that have survived the weather are scattered about the town. It is difficult in Redlands to scan the skyline in all directions and not see a single specimen. They are particularly numerous on the heights, often comprising small groves.

Today, with better advice from nurseries and landscape architects, the varieties chosen are of reasonable height and size. Usually they have beautiful bark — smooth and nearly white.

On the list of mistakes my first choice is the tree which nearly everyone erroneously calls "the monkey puzzle." That catchy name correctly refers to a tree of Chilean origin which has leaves so stiff and prickly that even a monkey could hardly climb it.

What Redlanders really mean is the bunya bunya tree, imported from Australia. Here it grows to great height, a picturesque tree with a domed top and very long branches.

Unfortunately, the bunya bunya produces cones which are larger than pineapples. If the tree happened to be angry at the owner — say for lack of care — it might drop a bomb on his head and kill him. The Santa Ana winds are thinning out the trees, but total eradication may not come for several decades.

Another tall tree which attracted the fancy of pioneer Redlanders was the deodar, a native of the Himalayas. An apocryphal story has it that A. K. Smiley ordered five hundred of them from a nursery in Paris. Checking the shipment upon arrival, he found one that was bad and would not pay for it. Whatever the truth may be, he planted a lot of them in Canyon Crest Park.

Hundreds of Redlanders followed suit in his day—and they still do.

When young this conical cedar is stunning for its shape, its gray-green needles and its forest character. Yet many folks seem to think of them as little Christmas trees. They will plant one in a small yard. In time, the cute little deodar reaches 80 feet high, with a very broad spread, and overwhelms the bungalow which it shades.

While many tall deodars have tips which bend over, others die back at the top or develop several erect branches in place of a trunk.

Like the eucalyptus, the deodar is usually in sight wherever you are—at least on the heights. The tops often profile against the sky, especially when you look west at dusk.

My personal favorites stand on either side of Center Street at Cypress. I call them "Judson and Brown" because it was at that intersection those gentlemen planned to locate a plaza. The plaza never got off the blueprints. For a time, Frank Brown had a home at the southwest corner, now occupied by Gerrard's market.

If the deodar looks like a forest tree to you, so will the redwood. Both are tall, conical in youth, and bear cones. The redwood foliage, however, is dark green while the trunk is made distinctive by soft, reddish brown bark.

That the deodar from the great Himalaya range of India and the redwood from the foggy coast of northern California will both grow in Redlands is remarkable. Here is a hint that an astonishing variety of ornamentals will tolerate our climate—cool in winter, hot in summer—if the roots can reach moisture. Hiatt found 158 different species along the streets.

Proof of the long survival of the sequoia sempervirens (redwoods) can be seen north from Brookside on Buena Vista and San Gorgonio. Those specimens are about 60 years old and look as if they are shooting for 100.

I wish I could observe that the coast redwood is THE official tree of California. Alas, the Legislature weaseled in adopting the tree-naming resolution and designated the sequoias, jointly. Thus they included the sequoia gigantea — the giant of Sequoia, Kings and Yosemite National Parks — with the sequoia semper-virens of Redwood National Park bordering the Pacific Ocean.

Many of the younger redwoods you see in Redlands are of varieties that have been improved for our use by plant breeders.

Contrasting with the forest-like look of the deodar and the redwood is the Italian cypress. This slender spire with dark green foliage is as formally dressed as a man in a tuxedo. No wonder it was favored for Italian gardens to complement fountains, stone walls, and statuary.

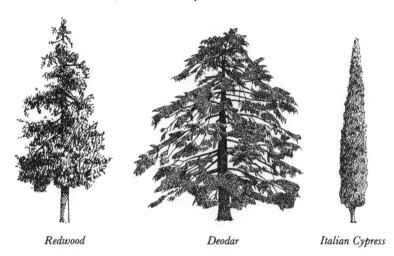

Redwood   *Deodar*   *Italian Cypress*

When planted close together in a line the Italian cypress will raise a 30-foot wall between one house and the next. You can find quite a few around town.

The city has used this variety sparingly along the streets. You have to hunt for examples, such as Norwood.

But the planters have used no restraint at all in Hillside Memorial Park. The stiff formality of the Italian cypress makes it appropriate for cemetery landscaping. So you'll find a veritable forest of 700 specimens.

While the deodar, redwood, cypress, pine and eucalyptus

keep Redlands green all the year round we have colorful trees that announce the beginning of a new season.

The impatient Bailey acacia won't wait for spring. It dresses itself in golden-yellow balls around January 20. You don't see it as a street tree because it has too short a life. Although the acacia requires pruning to give it a pleasing shape, it often grows wild on private property, crowding out other varieties.

You don't have to look at your calendar when the jacarandas bloom. Spring is well along and summer is appoaching. The tree is self-identifying by its showy clusters of lavender-blue flowers. They bloom in profusion. After weeks, the petals fall and spread a colorful carpet over the ground.

We ride on our luck when we plant jacarandas in Redlands. Native to Brazil, the tree is more at home in frost-free locations. Perhaps you have marvelled at their beauty in Mexico.

If Jack Frost spares a jacaranda when it is small, the tree ought to become well established. The large limbs of a mature tree may be killed by sustained cold, below 25 degrees, but given time the tree will recover.

The city has had an off-and-on policy about planting jacarandas along the streets. So many small trees were lost in a freeze that it was stricken from the official list in 1968. Memories fade. Personnel changes. The gorgeous flowering tree returned to favor.

If the jacaranda has established the right to proclaim the approach of summer, the oleander shouts when the school year is about over.

You can find the oleander along a few streets as a small tree with a ball of leaves and flowers standing on a slim trunk. But you would have to be blind to fail to see the hedges which abound through much of the city. The displays of white, pink and red are spectacular.

In the early days of Our Town the people went crazy over rose hedges. Some were more than a quarter mile long as on upper Serpentine and Alessandro.

Instead, we now have the bright, gay oleanders — a sight to

see. If Hillside Memorial Park is somber with Italian cypress inside, it is lavishly colored with flowers outside.

After the oleander has monopolized the stage for weeks, the crape myrtle blooms, often in such profusion of pink that the whole tree appears to be one flower. The lovely blossoms are crinkled and fringed.

Although this tree is small and you may not notice it during the winter and spring, you will have no difficulty finding it in midsummer when it is in bloom.

Crape Myrtle

The city is wild about crapes because they are small, easy to maintain and, in season, quite ornamental. Hiatt counted 6,288 of them — almost double the number of the runner-up, the California fan palm.

Crape myrtle has the merit of being interesting in three of the four seasons.

In the summer, the flower clusters splash the street-sides with lively shades of rose, pink and lavender.

In the fall, the small leaves seem to catch and hold bright sunlight in hues of red and copper.

In winter, the naked trees show their interesting structures, sheathed in bark which is smooth gray to light brown.

When in green leaf, they become inconspicuous.

Although the crapes are the more numerous trees, the liquidambars almost steal the fall show. Growing tall, they cloak themselves in maple-like leaves which turn brilliant crimson, orange and yellow. There are many of them.

Of the two varieties, Hiatt found the American sweetgum (1,619) to be the most numerous by far. His count of the Formosan sweet gum was only 152. The city could well plant more of the latter because they sustain autumn colors after most of their cousins have dropped their leaves.

The sweetgums have two peculiarities. You would suppose the name and spelling to be "liquidamber" with the reference being in English and pertaining to the color of the leaves. Not so. It's "ambar" with a second-syllable *a*, not an *e*. The Latin name refers to golden resin in the bark.

Unfortunately, the fruits are small, prickly balls. They harden, and, after the leaves are gone, either hang on the trees or drop. If they fall on a street where you walk at night, carry a flashlight or they may give you a fall.

The Indian laurel fig, an evergreen, stages no seasonal show. Hiatt located only 34 of them. Yet, you can't miss this handsome upright tree with rich green leaves. It grows in the planters on State and gives the street a friendly look. Until 1985 the foliage was dense and into this protective cover thousands of cowbirds would plunge at dusk. When the trees were opened by trimming, the garbage birds did not return.

Before ending this chapter, I must return to say a few more words about the palms.

Driving down Redlands boulevard from Ford to Cypress you find a smaller species, the Guadalupe, in the median.

In 1964 a freshman member of the City Council, Jack Cummings, learned that the park superintendent had a lot of these trees in a nursery. Could they be used to make the former Highway 99 attractive?

On one afternoon he offered his brainstorm to the Park Commission and won instant approval. In the evening he repeated his question at the Council meeting and scored again. He would say later: "That is one of the easiest things I ever did at City Hall and one of which I am most proud."

Canary Island Palm

Not yet mentioned along with the fan palms is the Canary Island date palm. You must learn to know it because so many of them (825) line the streets. The female is easily identified by the heavy clusters of orange (inedible) dates. All older trees are characterized by their height, their stout trunks, and the fountains of green that spray from the tops. The branch-like leaf is constructed like a feather. Typically it is 15 feet long.

This picturesque palm is out of fashion in Redlands because the dates are dangerous when they fall on a sidewalk. Also, they require expensive pruning, as do the California fan palms. You can spot very tall, stand-alone "canaries." They tell you that they were probably planted in the 1890s near a house that has since been torn down.

Finally, let's cope with the botanical names of the two most common palms in Redlands. You remember — the California fan palm for a mile on Cajon, and the Mexican fan palm in front of the Post Office.

Many people speak of a Washingtonia and believe they have designated a single palm. They haven't. Both have the same "first name."

The California is the Washingtonia filifera. The second word refers to the thread-like fibers that hang from the edges of the fronds.

The Mexican is the Washingtonia robusta. The second word was a poor choice because both of these trees are robust.

As to "Washington," opinion is divided. One school of botanists believes that the Father of Our Country is honored.

Another school of botanists insists that the name honors Colonel Henry Washington who, beginning in 1851, surveyed the San Bernardino Base Line and Meridian. Extending the grid of lines by which all property can be described, he did explore the canyons near Palm Springs where California fan palms grow wild. But botany was not his forte.

Whatever the origin of the botanical name may be — please, please — remember that we have two Washingtonias. Redlands would never look the same if all of them mysteriously disappeared.

Spectacles in the Sky

WE WHO LIVE IN REDLANDS can share with our forefathers the beauty of delicate clouds that seem to float in the blue sky. The heavenly show was here before we came, and it will go on and on after we are gone.

We can also watch some intriguing sights that were unknown before. Your grandfather never saw an airliner at night blinking its way across the town and sometimes seeming to collide with bright stars.

Nor has anyone before our time seen the immense loops of iridescent clouds which form when missiles are launched in the west at sunset. Even the rainbows of Nature are less awesome.

Yet, there is always something to see, to enjoy, to wonder about in our sky. Shall we start with the clouds?

For sheer beauty, Nature frequently gives us cirrus — pearly plumes, wispy filaments, fibrous streamers and little curls. You usually see them in clear sky, their bright white patterns contrasting with the blue of the heavens.

In stories of the sea you have read about them. Some mariners' lore may have stuck in your head: "Mares tails and mackeral scales make tall ships carry low sails."

Occasionally these ornamental clouds do signal an approaching storm. Lower and darker clouds follow them. But most of the time they foretell nothing. The Good Lord just creates them for us to enjoy in winter, spring, summer and fall.

If the scattered cirrus evolves into an unbroken overcast, take notice. By day, a large halo may encircle the sun. By night the moon will also wear a big ring.

Weather lore tells you that a halo around the sun or moon will bring rain. It can, but seldom does.

If you do much flying in airliners, you have probably noticed that you go up through the cirrus just before the plane reaches cruising altitude. They are the highest clouds of all. Over Redlands, that commonly means about 25,000 to 30,000 feet.

Although your airliner takes you right through the cirrus, you cannot see that they are composed of ice. The tiny crystals, beginning to fall like rain, create the filaments and plumes. They also make the sun and moon halos.

While you can see cirrus clouds nearly anywhere in the United States, we have two spectacular clouds that you would not see in flat country. They only form when north winds are blowing up over our mountains.

In the wake of a winter storm you may see a boa over the Rim of the World — the long ridge to our north. Named for a feathery, woman's scarf worn across the shoulder, it is really a lineal cloud that drapes over the summit. For a motorist driving from Crestline, at the west, to Running Springs and Snow Valley at the east, it seems to be an endless belt of fog. If he leaves the Rim and starts down the City Creek road, he will soon be in clear air.

The other cloud peculiarly associated with our mountains goes by a fancy name, "lenticular." That merely means that it has the shape of a lens — for example, a magnifying glass — when viewed edge on. The curves are so smooth they seem to have been formed by molten glass.

Lenticulars are most commonly seen to the east of Redlands, well to the south of the ridge over which the air is rising.

Created by what weather men call "a standing wave," they have two features in common with a waterfall. They stay in place. The moisture that makes them visible is ever-changing — in with the wind, out with the wind.

Although you won't find it in a meteorology book, we have a rare cloud you can only see when a cold, winter storm has just passed our way. This is a white banner that extends horizontally to the south from Mt. San Gorgonio. (Look due east to see it.) It is formed in this way:

A storm drops powder snow over the 11,499-foot peak. After

Lenticular Cloud, Mt. San Bernardino

the passage of the cold front, a fierce wind blows up the treeless, glacial bowls on the north slope and carries the crystals up and over the ridge. The white straight line extends into the San Gorgonio Pass. It's an awesome sight—one that makes you thankful you are not standing on the summit of Grayback.

*   *   *   *   *   *

Just as the mountains are responsible for some of our unusual clouds, they also put variety into our sunrises and sunsets. Moreover, it is a sporty proposition to guess exactly when and where on the skyline the moon will rise from wherever you happen to be watching. Let me explain about rise and set tables for the sun and moon. Of necessity they are based on a fiction that we have no mountains. Instead, you are supposed to be like a passenger on a ship at sea who can look across a "flat" ocean to an unobstructed horizon.

On the contrary, our mountains are like a fence. The sun or the moon must climb higher than the range to be seen. If the "fence" were level across the top, it would not be difficult to correct, say, the time of moonrise given in a table. But our skyline is a moderate sawtooth.

In December you may pause on State Street and look east to

see the full moon rise from near the top of our great pyramid, Mt. San Bernardino. The mountain will delay the moonrise about 32 minutes.

In June, the full moon will be far to the south, over the low profile of the Banning Pass. The delay will then be about 12 minutes.

The minute at which you see a sun or moon rise in Redlands will be later if you are closer to the mountains — say at Crafton Avenue — and earlier if you are farther out, say at Tennessee Street. In either location it will be earlier if the moon happens to rise from the Dollar Lake gap and later if from the top of Mt. San Bernardino.

Setting times are not as tricky as rising times, since the "fence" of hills and mountains to the west is lower and more even. The longest delay — about 12 minutes — comes in June when the sun sets over Mt. Baldy.

Seventh-Day Adventists, among all Redlanders, have the most consciousness of sunset times because they reckon the Sabbath from sunset on Friday to sunset Saturday. Being sensible people, they publish times in their weekly bulletin which are calculated for a flat horizon. No other kind would be practical.

* * * * * *

At 34 degrees North, we in Redlands are well situated to observe most of the stars and all of the planets. During the course of a year, we can see about 71 of the 88 constellations. The most famous one that hides below the San Timoteo Canyon hills is the Southern Cross.

Look straight out Orange at night and you will probably see Polaris, directly on the line of the street. It is found about one third of the way up from the Rim of the World to the zenith, the point directly overhead.

If you are familiar with the North Star, you find it by the "Pointers" in the Big Dipper. This constellation pivots around Polaris. When it goes down behind the mountains, can it be scooping water from a mysterious lake?

For months and months Venus is our evening star, so bright that you can see it in the west soon after sundown. Then it crosses the sun and becomes our morning star—out of sight, out of mind.

Of all the naked-eye planets, little Mercury is the most elusive. It bobs like a yo-yo, from one side of the sun to the other and never strays far from it. Many Redlanders have never seen it. Their best possibility comes when Mercury happens to be in the evening sky in April.

Alas, Mercury will be in the west and in that direction our visibility is the poorest. Westerly breezes bring haze from the ocean and smog from Orange and Los Angeles counties in the warm season.

Year by year, as the number of street lights increases, the night sky grows brighter and brighter. The dimmer stars are blotted out altogether. The Milky Way is not awesome. In "the good old days," stargazing was better.

*   *   *   *   *   *

Leaving astronomy for a moment, let's turn to the objects in the sky which are most noticeable—jet aircraft.

What are they? Why do they fly on those tracks?

As familiar as the sun and the moon are the cargo planes that come out of Norton AFB. Manufactured by Lockheed Marietta near Atlanta, Georgia, the company calls them StarLifters and the military calls them C-141's.

The pilots fly out on a prescribed course that takes them across Redlands. They climb for one mile and turn right on a compass heading of 130 degrees which is approximately southeast. After a couple of minutes you are likely to see one make a sweeping turn to the right. That means there was no conflicting traffic. By radio, a controller at Ontario gave the pilot permission to go west.

If you live in the Lugonia district of Redlands, you will often see a C-141 come in low from the west and make a left turn to land at Norton. This is most common in the afternoon when the prevailing westerly has become too strong (over 10 knots) — too much tail wind for an easy landing. The plane lands into a head wind.

When you see a number of C-141's taking off in rapid succession, you can bet they will soon gather into formation, fly down to Imperial Valley and practice dropping parachutes with attached cargo loads.

While the C-141's are so numerous and so obvious that they become boring, the airliners passing over Redlands are another story. If you served as a volunteer at the Army's aircraft observation post near Sunset Drive during World War II and the Korean War, you may be hooked for life. Your attention is invited by the sound of every jet that flies by.

If you happen to sit on your lawn on a Sunday evening in summer, you may see 20 airliners in an hour. They seem to be sliding along a single invisible wire. Sometimes they are separated by only two or three minutes.

The most curious thing about them is that virtually all are flying west. A bright child might ask: "Daddy. Do they all fly clear around the world before we see them again?" No, they don't.

This is the story.

Airliners fly paths in the sky that are as fixed as freeway routes on the ground. This is absolutely necessary to prevent collisions. The westbound tracks to Ontario and Los Angeles pass near, or over, Redlands. The eastbound routes lie well to the north and south of our town. That is the answer to the observant child's good question.

The jets that are going to LAX are the sportiest to watch. You first hear them, but can you see them? At night they are easy to spot, first appearing in the east as fixed stars and then becoming moving objects. They carelessly glide across the sky, not caring if they "hit" a star.

In daylight, however, they can be elusive, especially when the visibility is poor. At 13,000 to 18,000 feet a big airplane becomes a small object.

How fast are they flying? You can't tell from the ground. As a rule, the aircraft controllers are slowing them down. They may be going 400 miles per hour, but in heavy traffic they may be throttled back. When they have descended to 10,000 feet west of Redlands the speed limit automatically becomes 250 knots (nearly 300 mph).

*   *   *   *   *   *

Unless you can manage to live as long as Methuselah, your chances of seeing a full eclipse of the sun from Redlands are almost nil.

Yet, you might see the aurora borealis if you tried hard enough. That may seem improbable to you because many who have lived here for a long, long time will tell you they have never seen the northern lights.

So, let's review the elements of these events.

Two solar eclipses of some kind must occur every year. There may be five. However, a total eclipse of the sun is only visible along a path about 150 miles wide. The rule of thumb is that any particular place—say, Redlands—will happen to lie on that path about once in every 400 years.

The last time the sun was totally covered by the moon here was in 1806. We only know that from calculations made by astronomers since there was no literate person here at that time to observe the eclipse and make a written record of it.

However, Redlanders may see a partial eclipse when the path of totality is thousands of miles away. On July 10, 1972, the shadow raced across the ground from Alaska to southeastern Canada. As seen from here, the moon seemed to take a bite out of the sun amounting to about one-tenth of the area of the bright disk. That one was at noon.

On December 13, 1974, a partial eclipse was visible here but only at the very end of the show. The sun was just rising from Mt. San Jacinto, and, for a short time it was a peculiarly chewed-up crescent.

Eclipses of the moon, on the other hand, are not rare. From

1972 through 1982, three partial and three full ones were visible here. There is no particular Redlands aspect to lunar eclipses. They can be seen wherever the moon is above the horizon, which is over the half the earth. Of course, the sky must be clear.

Not to be outdone by Nature, man can stage a spectacle of dazzling beauty.

When a Minuteman missile is launched from Vandenberg AFB at sunset, contrails are left at extremely high altitude to the west of us. As to pattern, they suggest there is a great cowboy in the sky holding his lariat at arms length and twirling it to form a loop. The colors are iridescent; they might remind you of an abalone shell.

The loops become irregular as the minutes pass. When the sun fades out they still glow a greenish blue.

Sunset launches of Minutemen were common in 1969-70. Then I didn't notice another one until 1981.

There seems to be an invisible hand, however, that evens things up for people in different parts of the United States. In Southern California we may have missile contrails, but we rarely have a good show of the northern lights. In the Northeast, it's the other way around — no missiles, but many nights with the aurora borealis.

It's much a matter of geography. We are favored by our proximity to Vandenberg AFB; they are favored by being nearer to the magnetic pole, the point on the earth around which the aurora forms a halo. Your chances of seeing the lights would be about 25 times greater in Maine than in Redlands.

When the aurora does stage its most widespread displays, they are visible here unless the sky is overcast. For example, on April 12, 1981, red northern lights were visible from coast to coast and from the Gulf to Canada.

Colonel Bill Daniel and his son, Kenneth, happened to be at Running Springs, on top of the Rim due north of Redlands. They caught sight of the dazzling show after dinner at a cafe there. Coming down the City Creek grade, they could still see the aurora when they stopped at 3,700 feet elevation. Then they went below a cloud layer and could no longer see the red sky.

The aurora lights up most frequently at the peak of the 11-year sunspot cycle. The best period, just ahead, will be from 1990 until 1993.

Finally, in the rare spectacles class, we have Halley's Comet. I want to put something about its 1910 and 1986 returns on the record for any Redlander who can find a surviving copy of this book at the time of the next apparition in 2071.

I was not born until 1912, but every Redlander who was a child in 1910 swears that he remembers the comet. Nearly everyone who volunteers his recollections says that his father or mother held him up to see Halley. Quite a few seem to have been taken "upstairs" for a clear view.

I do not doubt their integrity, but I wonder about the reliability of every person's long-term memory. Having written the Grain of Salt column in the *Redlands Daily Facts* from 1942 until 1981, I can check the reliability of my own memory by reference to the files. I am no longer surprised when I find I have substituted one like event for another in recalling happenings of long ago.

What oldtimers never say anything about is the comet of January 1910. It was the bright one in that year. Although much talked about, newspaper accounts testify that Halley was rather disappointing to laymen.

As to the 1985–86 return of Halley, I personally observed him on 69 nights from November 13 to May 13. Most sightings were from my own backyard near the Redlands golf course. But I was only able to see him so often by photographing the sky, pinpointing the location of the comet from night to night and using astronomical binoculars.

At no time was Halley an easily seen, naked-eye object. If spotted with binoculars first, he could sometimes be seen without aid. Nor was there ever a tail that I could swear with certainty I had observed. And never mind that professional astronomers using a giant telescope in the Andes did get remarkable photographs of the Halley you would expect to see.

Several dozen people came to my house to have Halley pointed out. Nearly all were interested, otherwise they wouldn't have come. Those who had only a casual desire were disappointed. Usually they didn't say much. They were just let down. They had expected more. Those who spoke plainly were likely to make some remark such as Shakespeare's "Much ado about nothing."

There won't be any oldtimers when Halley returns again who can honestly boast: "I saw the comet in 1986. Gee, it was great!"

2

GETTING TO
KNOW REDLANDS

A Treasury of Redlands Books

So you want to know more about Redlands? That ought to be easy. Numerous books about the valley and the town have been published. But you may be frustrated because some are so scarce you can only read them at the A. K. Smiley Public Library.

Why is this so?

The market for local books is so small that there is no profit in publishing them. If the author must finance a book himself, he has no more copies printed than he hopes to sell within a few years. When the supply runs out, you can only lay hand on one by borrowing from a friend, finding one you can buy second hand, or going to the library.

Maybe a foundation could be established for the purpose of reprinting the books which are in constant demand, and keeping them on sale, year-to-year.

If Redlands is a new interest with you, here are the books to begin with.

Bill Moore's *Redlands Yesterdays* will spread before your eyes the pageant of the most romantic era of the city. Although this is primarily a photo album, the captions and text are carefully written. This curtain-raiser should whet your appetite for more. Because 5,000 copies were printed, it should be the least difficult to borrow. Don't look for it in stores, however. The issue was a sellout.

You will find the standard history of Redlands in Edith Parker Hinckley's *On the Banks of the Zanja*. She tells her story concisely and with the pride of a citizen who participated in community life for decades. A second printing somewhat increased the availability of the book. In 1960 she published a 36-page supplement covering the past decade. The title of this paperback is *Redlands – 1950–60.*

Dr. L. E. Nelson followed Mrs. Hinckley by a decade with *Only One Redlands.* Some people enjoy him for his never-failing sense of humor. They also like his eye for the feature angle in whatever he chooses to write about. But he employs a condensed style, reminiscent of an old-fashioned telegram. Some find him hard to read. Many copies were published by the Rike Foundation.

The list that follows is not in the usual order, that is, by author's name first and then alphabetic. Rather, it is chronological, the year being given first. This makes more sense when the subject is limited to Redlands history. You may not know the names of the authors, but the dates will give you valuable clues to the nature of the books.

1897 *Illustrated Redlands.* Redlands Daily Facts.
A priceless classic. Printed on glossy paper in large format (10 × 15). History while it was fresh. Redlands residents, their biographies and homes, illustrated with pictures of 124 houses; 234 portraits. Plus buildings, houses, and scenes.

1902 *Souvenir of Redlands, California.* F. C. Hoogstraat. Rawhide cover. Small format (8 × 10) Flowery prose laden with superlatives. 144 pictures, mostly of houses. 134 ads.

1902 *History of the San Bernardino Valley from the Padres to the Pioneers, 1810–1851.* Father Juan Caballeria of San Bernardino. Times-Index Press, San Bernardino. Small. Easy to read. Sympathetic to the mission founders and the Mexican-era rancheros.

1904 *Century Annals of San Bernardino County, 1769–1904.* Luther A. Ingersoll. Los Angeles. 887 pages. Excellent reference source on special topics such as citrus, water, railroads, pioneers. One chapter on Redlands. 80 Redlands area biographies scattered among 700. Ingersoll yields many historical nuggets if the organization of his book is carefully studied.

1906 *Pioneer Days in the San Bernardino Valley.* Mrs. E. P. R. Crafts. 214 pages. An account of pioneer life in the valley, with emphasis on schools, Sunday schools and churches. Amateurish but valuable for its personal reminiscences, especially of Crafton, adjoining Redlands to the east.

1914 *Eyes of the World.* Harold Bell Wright. First section flays the rich of Redlands for hypocrisy. Second section develops a wild melodrama in Mill Creek Canyon. A quaint period piece by a novelist of immense popularity in his day. The book was made into a movie. Wright is read most profitably for his excellent descriptions of our mountains.

1927 *Redlands, Twixt Mountains, Desert and the Sea.* Roger W. Truesdale and Bruce W. McDaniel. High school annual format. 88 photos of homes, schools, churches, gardens and civic buildings. 29 photos are of structures built in the 1920s, reflecting the popularity of the California "Spanish" style.

1938 *Golden Jubilee, Redlands, California - 1888-1938.* 215 pages. Historical chronology. 209 biographies with portraits. Many photographs — historic, current and of the Jubilee. Indexed.

1939 *Heritage of the Valley, San Bernardino's First Century.* George W. and Helen P. Beattie. San Pasqual Press, Pasadena. Intensively researched. This monumental work is THE authoritative history of the San Bernardino Valley from the coming of the white man to about 1870. Although not easy to read, "The Heritage" is a must for any student of the Mission, Rancho, Mormon and Civil War periods.

1946 *Frank Hinckley, California Engineer and Rancher - 1838-1890.* Edith Parker Hinckley. Saunders Press, Claremont, California.

Biography by his daughter-in-law. Hinckley came to California in 1863 and was an engineer and farmer in the north. Established a ranch in the Mission District (now in Loma Linda) in 1883; lived there with wife and 10 children until his death in 1890. Mirrors life of that period.

1951 *On the Banks of the Zanja – The Story of Redlands.* Edith Parker Hinckley. The Saunders Press, Claremont. Paperback supplement, *Redlands 1950–60.* See comment in opening text.

1954 *The Family Nobody Wanted.* Helen Doss. Little Brown, Boston. Carl and Helen Doss adopted 12 children of mixed races and sexes and raised them in Redlands. Strong in human interest, the book was adapted for television.

1958 *Redlands – Biography of a College.* Lawrence E. Nelson. Lively history of the first fifty years of the University of Redlands. Dr. Nelson served on the English Department faculty for 36 years, beginning in 1925.

1959 *The Autobiography of Robert Watchorn.* Edited by Herbert Faulkner West. Robert Watchorn Charities, Ltd. Oklahoma City. In Redlands, Watchorn gave the Lincoln Shrine to the city and a music building to the University of Redlands. An Horatio Alger story: boy coal miner in England, commissioner of immigration at Ellis Island, wealthy philanthropist. He made his fortune in oil.

1963 *Only One Redlands.* Lawrence E. Nelson, Ph.D. Two bindings: hardback; paperback of which hundreds were distributed by Redlands Community Music Association at the Bowl. Complements Mrs. Hinckley's sober *Banks of the Zanja.* 85 illustations. His fun-loving manner masks his scholarly research. See my comment at the beginning of this chapter.

1968 *The Prospect Park Book.* Erwin S. Hein, editor. Celebrating the 80th anniversary of Redlands and the acquisition of Prospect Park for the City. 241 pages. 2,000 copies. Richly illustrated with historical and contemporary photographs. A sequel to the Golden Jubilee book of 1938.

1969 *As the Spirit Moved Them: The Smileys—Alfred, Albert and Daniel.* Larry E. Burgess, Ph.D. Compact biography of the patron saints of Redlands. To understand Redlands, first understand the Smileys. This is the book.

1979 *Growing Up in Redlands.* Irene Hinckley Kupfer. Paperback. 171 pages. Personal memories, 1913–1928, of girlhood in the orange-growing period of the town. A graphic chapter describes difficult home life during heavy smudging in the groves.

1983 *Redlands Impressions.* Leo Politi, Los Angeles. Published by the Moore Historical Foundation. 20 pages. Paintings of five noted Redlands mansions by the illustrator of many children's books. The originals hang in the A. K. Smiley Public Library. Politi was inspired by the book to paint a mural for the children's room.

1983 *Redlands Yesterdays, a Photo Album—1870–1920.* William G. Moore. Published by the Moore Historical Foundation. 5,000 copies. 224 pages; 260 duotone photos. An instant classic. Text and pictures give the flavor of the most romantic era of Redlands. See comment at beginning of chapter.

1983 *Whose Emblem Shines Afar.* George H. Armacost, Ralph E. Hone and Esther N. Mertins. "A Commemorative Account of the University of Redlands for the Years 1945–1982." Carries forward Nelson's history of the first 50 years but not written in his lively style. Primarily of interest to the University of Redlands community.

1984 *Two Girls and a Kite or Adventures Around the Kite Shaped Track.* Edith Parker. Illustrated by Ethel Burt. Annotated by Larry E. Burgess, Ph.D. Jacket by Leo Politi. A collector's item. Parker (later, Edith Parker Hinckley) and Burt, Pasadena High School girls, took a railroad trip from Los Angeles to Redlands and back on the tourist route in 1899. The book reproduces Parker's travel diary, with sketches by Burt. Burgess explains and interprets for the contemporary reader.

1984 *San Bernardino County: Land of Contrasts.* Walter C. Schuiling. Produced in association with the San Bernardino County Museum Association, Windsor Publications, Inc., Woodland Hills, California. 206 pages. Many black and white pictures and 24 pages in color. Condensed history of the county. In the main, Schuiling weaves his limited Redlands material into his overall account. Back section is devoted to businesses and institutions, including six local to Redlands.

1985 *With a Grain of Salt.* Frank E. Moore. Published by the Moore Historical Foundation. A collection of 124 columns written while I was editor of the family-owned *Redlands Daily Facts,* 1942–1981. Varies widely in subject and mood.

1985 *Sunshine Citrus and Science.* Keld J. Reynolds. Published by the City of Loma Linda. Chronicles the growth of Loma Linda from the mission era to 1983. Carefully written and well researched. Various references to Redlands. Part of the Mission District—long considered to be in the Redlands area—is now within the corporate limits of Loma Linda.

1986 *Fun with Fritz—Adventures in Early Redlands, Big Bear and Hollywood with John H. "Fritz" Fisher.* Compiled by William G. Moore. Published by the Moore Historical Foundation. 2,000 copies. 126 pages. 109 duotone photos. Autobiographical—in word and in picture—of an adventurous spirit in the early automobile and early moving-picture eras.

1987 *The Pride and Glory of the Town — the Story of the A. K. Smiley Public Library.* Phyllis C. Irshay. Published by the City of Redlands as a centennial keepsake. 20 photos. Miss Irshay was the eighth Librarian, 1967–86. Her book is meticulously researched and well written. Rich in detail.

Streets, Alessandro to Zanja

IF YOU NOTICE our street signs, some of the names should pique your curiosity. For instance:

Alessandro. Was the road named for the hero of *Ramona?*

Oriental. Why do we have such a name in our Anglo/Spanish town?

Roosevelt. Which president—Teddy or Franklin?

If you want the answers, they don't come easily. Much has been written about the history of Redlands, but not about its street names. They are only mentioned in passing.

The story would be different if Our Town had a tradition of naming streets to honor citizens who have given special service. We don't. It is the School Board—not the City Council—that applies names to commemorate people: four elementary schools, three junior highs, and three high school buildings.

Of the Founding Fathers and Patron Saints, only E. G. Judson has a street, and his name applies to but half the total length. Frank E. Brown, Judson's locally famous partner, is missing from the roster. The Smiley twins are named by indirection. Grace Mullen, who created and established the Redlands Community Music Association, is left out.

As the municipality reaches the 100-year mark it is too late to improve our ways. The primary streets have been developed and named. Any proposal to rename a major thoroughfare would arouse the wrath of those who live on it. The City Council would have no stomach for such a controversy. Nor will City Hall even try to see that subdividers apply historic names. A splendid list was proposed a decade ago by the Preservation Commission. None has been used.

There are four unwritten rules of street naming:

(1) He who develops the land names the streets.

(2) If he doesn't supply names, his surveyor will.

(3) The proposed name will be vetoed by the Post Office, the Fire Department or the City Planning department if it is a duplication or would create confusion.

(4) Men are named by their last names, women by their first names. No one gets a first and last name.

Judson and Brown were the grandest name givers of all. When they acquired various parcels for their Redlands Colony there were no streets. They were the developers and Brown was the surveyor.

Brown planned the south-slope grid with boulevards at one-mile intervals and some at half-mile intervals. Their preliminary map included fifteen streets totalling 25 miles.

For east-west roads they showed a preference for trees and plants: Olive, Fern, Cypress, Palm, Chestnut, Walnut and Cedar. Whatever their horticultural intentions may have been in 1881, you'll find little or no connection today. There are no chestnuts on Chestnut or walnuts on Walnut.

Nor are many other Redlands names specific to particular streets. You have to enjoy the names for what you can read into them today.

It won't take you long to notice that some developers adopted themes. North of Colton and east of Orange are the long-established newspaper streets: Herald, Post, Sun, Tribune.

In the University of Redlands neighborhood are Berkeley, Campus, College, Occidental and University. Much later in the development of that area, another subdivider added Cornell, Harvard, Tulane and others.

Near the Smiley Heights tract are Robinhood, Nottingham and Sherwood. A surveyor, working later in that neighborhood, needed a single name and wrote "Kings Way" on a cul-de-sac. It stuck.

You might suppose the Mayflower had anchored in Plymouth Village instead of at Plymouth: Brewster, Alden, Standish, Carver.

For a bit of nostalgia, the members of the Chicago Colony gave Chicago names to the East Redlands district in which they built their homes and planted their orange groves: Wabash, Dearborn, Lincoln and LaSalle.

As developer of the Downtown business district, they chose State, or as the song, "Chicago" has it — "State Street, that Great Street." Surprisingly, the Colonists did not use the city name, Chicago, for any of their streets.

Developers have been known to name streets for themselves: Beauregard Crest and Caballero. They also honor their wives — Esther Way — and sweethearts. I can't identify the latter, but surely there are a number.

A few names just don't fit. Camino Real is one block long and dead ended. The namesake, El Camino Real, connected the California missions and was hundreds of miles long. The term meant "the government road" but is often translated erroneously as "the King's Highway."

Each name has two parts: Brookside (specific) and Avenue (generic). In many cases there are no criteria by which a choice of the generic word can be made. Here is the list in alphabetical order: Avenue, Boulevard, Bow, Circle, Court, Crest, Drive, Hill, Lane, Place, Road, Street and Way.

Redlands Boulevard is truly appropriate, but Sylvan Boulevard is ludicrous. Narrow and winding, it follows the course of the Zanja from Sylvan Park eastward to Dearborn.

When two or three streets are joined to make a continuous thoroughfare, a single name would make navigation easier for strangers.

Consider this boulevard which extends almost the total north-south width of the City: Orange, Cajon and Garden. A dictator could impose a uniform designation, but a City Council never could.

Citrus and Brookside are, in effect, a single street with an elbow at Eureka by the Post Office. The names will probably last as long as the city does. Yet, when Brookside passes Tennessee it becomes Barton Road and stays with that name through the cities of Loma Linda and Grand Terrace. Credit the late County Supervisor Wesley Break for that uniformity, negotiated at the time Barton was realigned through Loma Linda.

For amusement you might notice that some spellings are typographical errors: Barbra Lane. Anglos tend to have difficulty with Alessandro, which may sound Spanish, but isn't. Not one in a dozen can spell Chaparral (one *p* and two *r*'s). The signpost on Mariposa just goes along with the common error, Chapparal. Fortunately, Redlands has been spared from Tehachapi, a name that only residents of that town can spell.

Before we turn to specific names, a word about the protection of certain streets. In 1975 the City Council adopted a resolution designating Cajon as a Scenic Drive. The palm trees will be kept in their present locations. The curb-to-curb width will be retained. Curb parking would be banned as an alternative to widening.

Scenic designation has also been given to Center, Olive, Brookside, Highland, Canyon Road, Mariposa, Dwight, Sunset and the yet-to-be-constructed Santa Ana Bluffs Road.

Now, here are some interesting street names.

Alessandro. Starting at Crescent Avenue this street ascends to Hillside Memorial Park, then descends to San Timoteo Canyon. In 1890 it was improved by the new City government, making it the exit route from Redlands by carriage to the Alessandro Valley where Frank E. Brown was attempting to start a new town named Moreno. The name, Alessandro, was applied to a Santa Fe station in 1888 for the Indian hero in Helen Hunt Jackson's sentimental romance, *Ramona,* then at the height of its popularity. From the station the name spread to the valley in which Moreno is situated.

Alvarado. If there is poetic justice, this name was given to a Redlands street to honor Juan Bautista Alvarado, twelfth Mexican governor of California (1836–42). He is an important figure in California history. It is significant locally that he made the grant of the Rancho San Bernardino to the Lugo family in 1842. The grant included much of the land extending from

Colton through Redlands to Yucaipa.

Brookside. The "brook" was the Mill Creek Zanja which flowed parallel to the avenue in the vicinity of Tennessee. The thoroughfare was developed with trees down the center to the City Limits. During one period a streetcar line was also situated in the median. The name Brookside was also used by the Vache family as a brand name for the wine they made when they leased Dr. Ben Barton's vineyards adjacent to the Asistencia and the Zanja. They took the term with them when they developed a vineyard and winery on the floor of San Timoteo Canyon below Community Hospital. A railroad siding serving the winery was called Brookside. (see Fern)

Cajon Pass

Cajon (Kah HOHN). Judson and Brown chose to name their main boulevard up the slope of the Redlands Colony for the great Cajon Pass. This gateway from the coastal plain to the Mojave Desert, as seen from Redlands, is the low saddle between the San Gabriel and San Bernardino ranges. The name comes from the Spanish word for box. The Californios applied it to any canyon they regarded as being box-like at the head.

Center. Judson and Brown gave the name to Center Street when it was only a line on their preliminary map. They intended to create a plaza on it at Cypress Avenue. The plaza was never built. The name Center remained, although Cajon turned out to be the central route from the business district to Redlands Heights.

Church. Pioneer settlers in Lugonia built a Congregational church at the corner of the Terrace and Church, thus giving the street its name. Dedicated in 1883, the "carpenter's Gothic" chapel was used for only 15 years. It was the first church within the boundaries of Redlands, established by incorporation of the city in 1888. Four Lugonia district streets were located on section lines — Wabash, Judson, Church and Texas. Only Church, however, has a counterpart in East Highlands on the north side of the Santa Ana wash. That section terminates, at the north, on private land and on a ridge which appears to be a surface expression of the San Andreas Fault.

Colton. The avenue, like the City of Colton, was named for David D. Colton, junior partner of the Big Four in building the Central Pacific Railroad. In 1875 the Southern Pacific line, building eastward from Los Angeles, reached the Slover Mountain Colony. SP renamed the settlement Colton in honor of its vice president. (David Colton was U.S. Senator David Broderick's second in the pistol duel, 1859, in which Broderick was killed by California Chief Justice David S. Terry.) The single avenue name was used for decades for the entire length from the Crafton Hills to the Santa Ana River near Colton. For the renaming west of Alabama Street in 1963, see the entry for Redlands Boulevard.

Eureka. It is named for the California motto which appears on the State Seal. Archimedes (287–212 B.C.), the great Greek geometrician, used the exclamation, "I have found it," when he discovered the principle of specific gravity. Eureka Street developed at intervals in residential segments. Each is in the architectural style in fashion at the time. The business and commercial section, from Brookside to Colton, became a thoroughfare after 1962 because of the exit onto Eureka from the then-new Interstate 10.

Ford/Judson. Harry Ford, prominent Redlands banker, owned and lived in an orange grove at the southern end of Ford Street. The boulevard developed from his ranch road. E. G. Judson, cofounder of Redlands, was the City's first mayor. The street is north of the Redlands Colony, and therefore was not named by him or his partner, Frank E. Brown, but by others to honor him. Ford/Judson was not a continuous street until subdividers created the link from Highland to Citrus. Faced with the proposal of giving a single name to the boulevard, the City Council waffled. Thus the name is Judson, north from Citrus, and Ford, south from Citrus. The City Council planned to extend Ford through Garden Hill to Garden and acquired property on the right-of-way. The project was stalled by an unfortunate recommendation of the then-new Public Works Advisory Commission. I frequently take evening walks in which I encounter motorists who are totally lost at what appears to them to be the dead-end of Ford. They are victims of the uncompleted project. When I am king, the link will be constructed immediately.

Lugonia. The governor of Mexican California granted the Rancho San Bernardino to the family of Don Antonio Maria Lugo. It extended from Colton through Redlands to Yucaipa. The Lugos sold their lands to the Mormons in 1851. Within the present City of Redlands, settlement began in the northern section, from about Colton Avenue to the Santa Ana Wash. In 1887 a new school district was created there. C. R. Paine, who had been county superintendent of schools, suggested the name, Lugonia. This came to be applied not only to the school, but to anything that needed a name—church, water company, packing company and post office. Emphasis on the name began to diminish after 1888 when Redlands was incorporated and Lugonia became a district within the municipality. The Lugonia Elementary School and Lugonia Avenue are the most prominent carriers of the name today. Lugonia is not only a major east-west street but from Orange to Wabash, it also doubles as State Route 38. This route extends for 56 miles to Bear Valley. Going eastward from Orange, the name Lugonia ends at Wabash. The boulevard is clearly called Mentone Boulevard in the business district of Mentone, while it is variously signed to the eastward as State Route 38 and as Mill Creek Road.

North Place. This short, narrow street extends east from Center a block north of Cypress. Judson and Brown so named it because it was to be the north boundary of their plaza at Center and Cypress—the one they planned but never built. It is a relic of their dreams.

South Avenue. When the Mexican government ceded California to the U.S., the Americans promptly initiated their standard system of surveying to establish secure land titles. From a point on Mt. San Bernardino, Col. Henry Washington ran a base line to the Pacific Ocean and to the Colorado River and a meridian from Death Valley to the Mexican border. From these lines, surveyors laid out townships, six miles square. Redlands lies in the third township west of Mt. San Bernardino and the first one south of the base line. South Avenue is on the south boundary of our township, and Base Line is the north boundary. It is curious that three Redlands elementary schools are on township streets —Cram, Base Line; Kimberly, South Avenue; and Crafton, Wabash Avenue. The fourth township avenue is Mountain View. Victoria School is situated about half-mile west of it.

Orange. The name is old, predating Judson and Brown's first preliminary map of their Redlands Colony. Need I say that it is appropriate for the main north-south boulevard of Downtown and Lugonia in a city that once claimed to be "The Navel Orange Center of the World"? While we have a Valencia Street, namers have shied away from Navel. This orange does have one end that suggests the human "belly button"; thus, the descriptive but unattractive name. Confusion sometimes arises between this thoroughfare—Orange Street—and Orange Avenue, westerly from Tennessee.

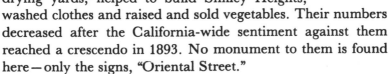

Oriental. Redlands Chinatown was located on this street which parallels Redlands Boulevard, westerly from Eureka. Behind the name lies the story of the men who came here as domestic servants, and more importantly as common laborers. They picked fruit and grapes, worked in the fruit drying yards, helped to build Smiley Heights, *Chinaman* washed clothes and raised and sold vegetables. Their numbers decreased after the California-wide sentiment against them reached a crescendo in 1893. No monument to them is found here—only the signs, "Oriental Street."

Redlands Boulevard. A highway to carry traffic through the City evolved between 1915 and 1946. This came to be called The Ocean-to-Ocean Highway and then U.S. 70 and 99. It was created by linking existing streets and by the construction of some all-new alignments. Minor confusion existed between street names and the overall highway numbers. The route was turned over to the City and the County in their respective territories when it was superseded by the freeway, Interstate 10, in 1962. County Supervisor Wesley Break seized the opportunity to rename the entire eight miles. In 1963 he was successful in gaining acceptance for "Redlands Boulevard." Included were Beacon Street and part of Central Avenue in Redlands, and all of Colton Avenue west of Alabama. The eight-mile boulevard now lies within Redlands, county territory, Loma Linda, and a small part of San Bernardino. Historically, Redlands Street (not Redlands Boulevard) ran on the diagonal from what are now the corners of Ford/Citrus to Fifth/Dearborn. The City Council expected all of it to disappear as the land through which it passed was subdivided. However, a short block remains, southeast from Highland to the Moore Junior High campus.

Reservoir/Roosevelt. Water for the Redlands Colony was impounded in a reservoir. The site is now recognizable as a shallow bowl in Ford Park. The name was attached to the straight street below it, from Highland to Citrus and, also, to the portion above it in Reservoir Canyon. The straight portion was renamed in about 1920 in honor of Theodore Roosevelt who toured Redlands by carriage in 1903. The section above Ford Street, closely following the freeway, retains the original name. Because Roosevelt is narrow and used to have a high crown, it is difficult to imagine that it was a link in a transcontinental highway. Moreover, it passed right through the high school campus between two large buildings. The noise of trucks backfiring as they came down the grade in compression was annoying, but the threat to pedestrian students from runaway trucks was downright frightening. The City tried to correct these problems by constructing a diagonal bypass just above the campus. This removed the daily traffic, but left the alarming problem of the runaways. In 1943 City Engineer George Hinckley built a pond, 300 feet long, on the unused line of Roosevelt in hopes that out-of-control trucks would plunge into it and stop harmlessly. However, drivers feared drowning more than overturning and swerved to miss it. No truck ever went into the water. The problem was solved in 1946 when the state built the stretch of Redlands Boulevard from Fern to Ford Street on an entirely new alignment. Roosevelt Road was no longer a section of the highway.

San Mateo and San Timoteo. The names are occasionally confused because of their similiar sound. San Mateo is the street from Highland to Brookside. The name of the apostle, Saint Matthew, was repeatedly used by the Spanish in California. Why the Americans, Judson and Brown, applied it to their most westerly street is unknown. San Timoteo Canyon lies just beyond the crest of the Redlands slope and a portion of the City is in it. A rancho of this name was owned by Mission San Gabriel and included the site of El Casco in the upper canyon.

Serpentine. Descriptively named for the portion from Sunset Drive to Highland, it is one of a set of streets located in the bottoms of meandering, shallow ravines on the Redlands Heights.

Smiley Heights. At the summit of their private park, A. H. and A. K. Smiley built a scenic road and named it, appropriately, Canyon Crest Drive. Riding in a carriage, a tourist could see into both San Timoteo Canyon and the San Bernardino Valley. Smiley Heights Drive, a modern feature, is at a lower elevation and was engineered as a residential street.

Sunset. A long, scenic loop on the crest of the Redlands Heights, it was completed in 1902 by connecting new construction to existing roads. A. H. Smiley was a central figure in the project. His efforts were so exhausting that he never recovered and died in January, 1903. The carriage road had many curves, some sharp, and was designed to give ever-changing views of the valley and mountains. Upon completion in May 1902, the committee asked the public to suggest apt names. "Sunset" was chosen. In 1936 the county paved dirt sections and built Panorama Point, overlooking Crystal Springs.

Terracina. It was named for the Italian coastal city, north of Naples, by promoters of a would-be city in the late 1880s. Imposing Hotel Terracina stood on the present site of Community Hospital until it burned. For a time a street railway line reached Terracina Boulevard by way of Olive Avenue. The boulevard and adjacent land were not in the original city limits of Redlands.

The Terrace. Located atop a fault embankment, the street is higher than Colton which it closely parallels from Sixth to Church. It developed as the choice residential street of Lugonia in early days. The Terrace Villa Hotel was converted by mining millionaire A. G. Hubbard into a noteworthy mansion. The Hotel Terracina and the Terrace Villa Hotel are often confused. In Redlands, Spanish street names are preceded by the article, "la," but English street names are not prefaced with "the." The Terrace is the exception.

Interstate 10. Eastward from the Octopus, through Loma Linda and Redlands, the freeway has no other name. Many maps indicating the locations of new subdivisions in Redlands have erroneously labelled it "San Bernardino Freeway." The local section was opened to traffic in 1962, with three lanes on each side of the median.

Downtown Landmarks

THE TRIANGLE, JUST A MEMORY

For sixty years any Redlander would know what you meant if you said: "I'll meet you at the Triangle."

Today, the reply might be: "The Triangle? What's that?"

Yes, the most famous landmark in the town has shrunk so much that only the oldtimers are aware of it.

This story goes back to the early 1880s when Frank E. Brown laid out the south side street grid on an angle to the Lugonia grid. This left an orphan triangle of land bounded by Cajon, Citrus and Orange Streets.

Two pioneer owners of the little plot provided that it was to be used "as a public fountain and watering place." The Humane Society installed a stone horse trough which served for decades.

A later grant deed provided that the Triangle was given to the City of Redlands on the condition that "The grantee shall not at any time manufacture or sell intoxicating liquors, distilled or fermented, on said land."

Because of its prime location, the Triangle naturally attracted improvements. It was there that the Junior Order of United American Mechanics raised the Liberty Pole in 1895. It was there that City dignitaries assembled in 1916 for the ceremonial planting of the California Live Oak which is still there.

Festooned with colored lights, the oak became our municipal Christmas tree. When someone suggested community singing on Christmas Eve, the Triangle was automatically chosen as the convenient place.

In World War II it was at the Triangle that Redlanders gathered for War Bond rallies, always featuring an out-of-town celebrity.

The Triangle

Later, curbstone campaigning became a brief fashion. Congressman Richard Nixon, seeking to become a senator, spoke to a modest crowd there.

When Jimmy Roosevelt came to town to campaign against Governor Earl Warren, he parked his big van on the Cajon Street side of the Triangle.

The early evolution of transportation in Redlands had bolstered the Triangle's identity as the foremost landmark in the heart of the town.

By 1909 the electric street car systems had developed to their maximum mileage. From the Triangle, trolleys clanged away in four directions — east and west on Citrus, south on Cajon and north on Orange.

A decade later, the Ocean-to-Ocean Highway exposed the Triangle to the view of all who came down Citrus and turned out Orange.

But as the evolution of transportation continued, the fortunes of the Triangle reversed.

Gradually, the street car lines shrank in mileage and finally ceased to operate.

The automobile, which had driven them out, needed room downtown as close to stores and offices as possible. The Cajon Street side was closed to traffic and incorporated in a municipal parking lot.

From the diminished Triangle, the Liberty Pole was moved south about half a block.

Next came the telephone company with a pressing need to expand the Redlands exchange. It is in the nature of a telephone system that it must be centralized as close to the city center as possible. A deal was made. The municipal parking lot would be relocated nearby and the new telephone building would nudge up to the Triangle.

The once-proud landmark remains in the memory of long-time Redlanders, while the actual Triangle has sunk into obscurity.

Today, the only prominent reminder of yesteryear is City Gardener Bob Adams' venerable oak tree, casting its shade over a small patch of bare ground. Oh, yes—there are still benches facing in three directions. But they don't have their former attraction for the old boys who used to sit there every day watching the world go by.

The geography of Redlands predestined the Triangle to a period of glory and to ultimate decline.

THE LIBERTY POLE—TALL AND PROUD

Two centuries ago a seed from a Douglas fir tree in Oregon fell on a forest floor, germinated and took root. It grew for about one hundred years. Then, in 1895, it was cut down, debarked, finished and shipped from Eureka to San Diego by schooner.

At the dock, it was loaded on a Santa Fe flat car in two sections and shipped to Redlands. From the railroad siding the pieces were hauled by horse and wagon to the chosen site, The Triangle, at Orange and Citrus.

Using a derrick brought from San Bernardino, David Morey bossed the erection of the very tall mast. His name has become locally famous in modern times because so many people know of the gingerbread mansion he erected for himself and his wife on Terracina at Olive.

Some young men who watched the job, in telling about Morey's difficulties with the derrick, recalled the story a generation later for the *Facts*. They referred to him as an "old sailor." He really wasn't. It is possible that the misnomer contributed to the false legend that the fir was a ship's mast before it was a flagpole.

While the upper section was being raised and secured to the lower section, there was grandiose talk of placing a crown of twelve arc lights at the top. Apparently the Redlands Light and Power Company was less than enthusiastic. The scheme died aborning.

The work at the Triangle began on August 31, 1895, and by September 5 the community of 3,500 souls was ripe for a celebration. The Liberty Pole was dedicated with sky rockets, marching National Guardsmen and stirring band music.

From the streets people crowded into the nearby Academy of Music for an exhausting program of rhetoric.

One orator, Halsey Allen, lauded the Junior Order of United American Mechanics whose Redlands council planned, financed and carried out the project. Oddly, little was said about the history of Liberty Poles.

The original Liberty Tree was an elm in Boston, a rallying place for Sons of Liberty who met under its boughs, denounced British oppression, drank toasts, sang songs and hanged unpopular officials in effigy. British soldiers in 1775 cut it into 14 cords of firewood.

The best known Liberty Pole was erected in New York City (1766), with approval of the royal governor in celebration of the repeal of the Stamp Act. Raised in harmony, it soon became the focus of brawls between British soldiers and Liberty Boys, attended by lively street fights and bloodshed.

As the years went by the Redlands Liberty Pole became such a familiar fixture that it was taken for granted.

In 1959 Lee and Mary Ann Quinn showed up at City Hall and immediately got the job of painting the staff. They brought new perspective. Steeplejacking was their life, from Maine to Hawaii, from California to Alaska.

Lee told me that in roaming about the U.S. he had painted numerous staffs which had been raised by the Junior Order of Mechanics. They had always called them "Liberty Poles."

"Your flagpole ranks among the highest in the nation," Mary Ann added. "It is 114 feet tall. There are some taller — 120 feet.

"We don't find many more like this except in New England. That's because the coastal towns often used the masts of old clipper ships.

"Some of those masts are pretty far gone. In Rhode Island my husband put his arm in one clear up to his elbow, it was so fat and so hollow."

Testing our pole with an ice pick, at eye level, Lee concluded that it might be prudent at some time to shorten it and reset it. That action was not long in coming, but for an indirect reason.

The City created a parking lot, west from the Triangle, and closed Cajon Street. Crowded in the new landscaping, the pole needed a better location. After much discussion, the present site at Cajon and Vine was agreed upon.

One perceptive Redlander had earlier brought back the idea from Mazatlan, Mexico, that a base might be built and surfaced with mosaics. Alas, the love of public art found below the border was not found here.

Instead, a strictly engineering approach — maximum support for the pole — was taken. A block of tapered concrete, as high as man's eye, was cast around a steel casing and given a gunite surface.

On June 7, 1963 — with a mobile crane lifting — the pole was cut with a chain saw, five feet above the ground level. Then the lower portion was given anti-termite treatment. Although the total job required two hours, the crane and its load moved 200 feet to the new location in 10 minutes.

According to the public works director, the new height of the Liberty Pole had been reduced to 106 feet.

On the stump which remained at the Triangle, Professor Frederick (Fritz) Bromberger counted 101 rings within the 17-inch diameter. He said: "That means that if the tree was logged in the same year the staff was erected in Redlands, it started to grow in about 1794."

The newly located staff did not have a crown of lights as the Junior Order of Mechanics had hoped for in 1895. Instead, a spotlight was placed on the front of City Hall and directed to illuminate the flag by night. Thus, our flag is never taken down except during foul weather.

Vicious Santa Ana winds can so tatter a flag that it will have to be replaced in seven weeks or so. In fair weather the cotton bunting is good for six months.

As to the pole itself, the elements never bring disaster. On July 23, 1986, a story was published that lightning struck the staff and knocked out the City's phones for an hour and a half. During my fifty years of newspapering in Redlands that had never happened before. Could it really be true?

Inspecting the pole from top to bottom, I could see no evidence of a lightning strike. The steel-wire halyard did not have any unusual appearance. After inquiring among people in City Hall, I concluded that the story had originated with speculation by a telephone executive from Pomona who needed an alibi for the failure of the system.

Our venerable Liberty Pole awaits a centennial celebration on September 5, 1995. Let's make it a good one.

A SALUTE TO PRESIDENT MCKINLEY

McKinley Monument

In September 1901, all Redlanders were stunned by the news. An anarchist had shot the President of the United States at Buffalo. In eight days, William McKinley was dead.

Only six months earlier McKinley gave Redlands its greatest day of glory. He made his "official entry" into California here and was given a tremendous welcome.

Sentiment spontaneously arose for memorializing the martyr in some way. At first, there was grandiose talk about a large monument, but when it came down to putting cash on the line the proposals became more realistic.

The final outcome was that a bust — not a full figure — was purchased and eventually placed on a granite pedestal. Mr. McKinley, in bronze, looks down on everyone who walks from Eureka Street into the Bowl.

In retrospect it is well that the movement of 1901 turned out the way it did. The sculpture by William Couper of New York is strong and of just the right size. The wording on the granite face is masterful, saying no more and no less than was intended. This is the way it reads:

"William McKinley — Patriot, Statesman, Martyr.

"As President of the United States he visited this city on the eighth day of May, 1901 –

"And the freedom of the state was here tendered to him by the Governor of California.

"As a tribute to the man, and a record of the event, this memorial was erected by the citizens of Redlands."

Anyone who looks closely will find a postscript to this inscription. It is cast in bronze and affixed to the base of the monument. It reads:

"Unveiled May 7, 1903 on occasion of the visit of Theodore Roosevelt, President of the U.S. Dedicated Memorial Day under auspices of Bear Valley Post, 162, G.A.R."

The unveiling was without ceremony. Although it would have been appropriate for President Roosevelt to officiate, there simply wasn't time during his crowded visit. Moreover, TR was a Spanish-American War hero. Members of the Grand Army of the Republic counted McKinley as one of their very own. He enlisted for the Civil War at age 18, rose to captain and was breveted a major.

TR's carriage drive did take him by the McKinley bust. The *Facts* reported: "The President's attention was called to the monument. While the carriage slacked up, President Roosevelt rose and uncovered his head in respect for his predecessor. Others followed his example."

The ceremony on Memorial Day included two orations, with much rhetoric, as was the custom of the time.

FOUNTAIN, BENCH AND BRICKS

If you have time to kill while you are downtown, you may enjoy walking around to see three things — the Safety Hall Fountain, the Stillman tile bench, and the name bricks on State Street.

The Safety Hall Fountain

Jubilees of the City of Redlands kindle a good spirit. Citizens become unusually friendly toward their community and are sometimes moved to express themselves in some tangible way.

Pausing in front of the Safety Hall Fountain, at the corner of Citrus-Brookside and Eureka, you will find this is so by reading this text on the plaque: "In Commemoration of the 75th Anni-

versary of the City of Redlands. Donated by Redlands
City Employees Association
[and] Redlands Horticul-
tural and Improvement Society. 1963."

Safety Hall Fountain

When you walk west on
Citrus, passing the Mall, you
see the fountain directly
ahead. The spray, being in
motion, catches your eye. As you approach you become aware of
the colorful flower bed surrounding the large circle. Blue-and-
white is the color scheme — first, the white spray and the blue
water in the pool, and again in the small-tiles mosaic on the low
wall of the basin.

You are free, of course, to throw a penny in the water and
make a wish. But a cent doesn't go far any more. Perhaps you
would have better luck with a dime or a quarter.

The Stillman Bench

Spanish themes have been architecturally expressed in many
Redlands buildings, but the one authentic touch of Spain is the
bench on Fourth Street by the A. K. Smiley Public Library.

You will not learn this, however, from a tile on which is
printed: "Leland Stillman Memorial Bench. 1951."

Lee, as he was commonly called, worked in decorative tile as
a hobby. While touring Spain with his mother, he took a fancy
to a set of tiles, bought them, and had them shipped to the Stillman home in Redlands.

For health reasons he went to Arizona, bought a ranch near
Prescott and became a cattleman. He died there in 1937.

His mother, Mrs. Leland Stillman (Sr.) offered the Spanish
tiles to the City. In 1947 the Beautification Committee proposed
to the Council that an ornamental bench be made with them.

Stillman Bench

The plan germinated slowly. In 1951 Mrs. Stillman had the seat made.

It would have been better if the full name—Leland Stanford Stillman, Jr.—had been used on the bench.

Lee was the son of Leland Stanford Stillman, who became a New York attorney. He was also the grandson of J. D. B. Stillman.

From the East, Dr. Stillman came by squarerigger around Cape Horn to California. Here, he made medical history in Sacramento and then in San Francisco.

He became a friend of Leland Stanford, was personal physician to him for a time, and named a son after him. In 1879 Senator Stanford engaged E. Muybridge to make his famous movie-like photographs of a running horse. Dr. Stillman, after making a careful study of the anatomy of a horse, wrote the monograph to go with the pictures.

In pre-Redlands days he came to the Lugonia district, built his home and established a ranch on what is now the University of Redlands Campus. He raised grapes for making both raisins and wine. Unfortunately, he died in 1888 just as the City was incorporated.

If you have now seen the Safety Hall Fountain and the Stillman Bench, you have a quite different assignment ahead:

The Name Bricks on State Street

In 1985 the Redevelopment Agency was giving State Street a new/old appearance by replacing the cement sidewalks with red bricks, bordered by brown bricks.

The agency sponsored a gimmick for the financial benefit of Town Center Corporation, a booster of Downtown business.

For $25, anyone could buy a brick. That is, whatever he chose within the letter limits, would be imprinted on it at the kiln. This proved to be wildly popular. 2,500 were bought.

For a Founder's Brick, the price was $1,000. Eighteen were ordered. As it turned out, the bricks which were first delivered to the Agency lacked class; so did an upgraded set which followed on reorder. In the end, nothing short of bronze would do. These plaques were mounted as a set on the State Street wall of Hales Park.

To find a particular brick you have to walk up and down State Street, looking and occasionally chuckling. The inscriptions comprise a medley of valentines, tombstones, bumper stickers, familiar sayings, advertising, personalized license plates, gags and greeting cards.

My favorite is the droll, humorous salutation: "See you on The Hill." The Hill, of course, is Hillside Memorial Park.

HALES PARK, DOWNTOWN OASIS

Walking up State Street on a hot summer day, a Redlander comes to a welcome oasis — Hales Park.

The broad leaves of the sycamore trees cast shade over the green lawn. Water bubbles from the Nollar Fountain and cascades over the brick rings. A mother, carrying a baby, pauses to sit on a bench and rest. Brown baggers eat their lunches at the picnic tables.

The peacefulness of the scene belies the small tempests that have marked the evolution of the park.

Hales Park

For more than half a century this site at the northeast corner of Fifth Street was overwhelmed by a tall building. Various tenants occupied it through the years. From 1903 until about 1918 the Redlands Post Office was on the ground floor. Later it was favored by furniture stores because it had large space on three floors.

With time the structure deteriorated and became functionally obsolete. It was torn down.

The brick wall on the adjoining building was exposed to view for the first time in decades. On it were painted signs. One, of modest size, identified the location of the Redlands Bakery. Much larger were: "Western Star Soap" and "Mermaid Queen German Family Soap."

The owners of the Sliger Music store felt that the wall should be painted. But they ran into a buzz saw. Customers held strong but divided opinions. One school insisted that the signs were ugly; another insisted that they were not only quaint but historic gems. An informal poll, with secret ballots, showed opinion was about 50-50.

Agitation began for a mini-park on the glaringly vacant site.

The City decided to proceed and engaged an Orange County landscaping company, P.O.D., to prepare a plan. At that time — 1978 — P.O.D. was already at work on a master plan for Prospect Park.

Hard-pressed for funds, the City did not want to be stuck with the cost of watering and mowing a lawn. Most of the ground would be bare except for the paved area under the pavilion. This dominant structure was conceived by Dwayne Blossom of P.O.D. and built at the outset.

The City Council asked the citizenry to suggest names. None of the nominations was embraced with enthusiasm. The least inappropriate — "Central Park" — was accepted.

Nor was there applause for Blossom's starkly modern pavilion. Criticism of it did not subside until the natural wood finish of the upper structure was softened with brown paint.

Although the sycamore grove, taking on height, made the mini-park more attractive, the bare ground was bleak. The City Council caved in and ordered grass.

In October 1978 Worden Nollar died of a heart attack, quite unexpectedly. For 40 years he had been a teacher, coach and administrator in the schools of Redlands and Yucaipa. He was a tireless worker in the Boy Scouts and was a member of the Park Commission. In whatever role, there was beneath his sometimes gruff exterior a man who cared about people.

Worden's friends immediately began to solicit funds for a memorial fountain. A ready-made one was purchased and installed but vandals destroyed it. The substantial replacement features a bubbling burst of water which cascades over 11 tiers, each ring larger than the one above. It is quite appealing.

In 1983 Edwin R. Hales, a native of Redlands and one of its most active civic leaders for years, died. He had been a member of the City Planning Commission for 36 years, including 33 as Chairman. There was a spontaneous and quick reaction: rename Central Park in his honor. Opinion was so unanimous that the Council scarcely needed to formalize the name change.

Drastic work by the Redevelopment Agency in 1985 to

improve the appearance of State Street brought further features to make Hales Park more interesting.

In tearing up the blacktop in the street, construction crews exposed the original red paving. The bricks dated to 1892. Seven hundred were selected and laid in a pattern adjacent to "Founders Square" on the south side of Hales Park.

At the very corner of State and Fifth, a low, unique monument was placed. It was fashioned from sections of granite, a fact that a surmounting plaque failed to explain. Without public notice or attention, it was removed. What was the real story here?

In the 1890s the City Council decreed that the curbs on State Street would be made of granite. The stone segments were still in place in 1985. They were removed during the Redevelopment project. Sections were resurfaced to bring out the natural beauty of the rock. Then they were cut and shaped so that 13 pieces could be vertically assembled to form this short-lived monument.

While the drastic Redevelopment work was going on, some citizens hoped that the faded soap signs on Sliger's wall would be cleaned off. To their dismay, the noon Rotary Club hired a man to revive the dim white letters in a lively shade of yellow.

There's nothing quite like Hales Park elsewhere in town.

Monuments and Gates

GUACHAMA, WHERE IRRIGATION BEGAN

Guachama Monument

Plymouth Rock is one of the most celebrated monuments in America. According to legend, the Pilgrims stepped on this boulder when disembarking from the Mayflower. Then began the founding of the first permanent white settlement in New England.

If there is such a thing as poetic justice, we, too, should have a "Plymouth Rock." It is the place where agriculture — the basis of our civilization — began.

The site is four miles west of Redlands on Mission Road. A motorist can find it easily because power transmission lines cross over the boulevard at that point.

Alas, Guachama is not glorified with Grecian columns in the style of Plymouth Rock. Rather, there is a modest cement monument on the north side of the road.

The undisputed fact is that the Spanish padres of Mission San Gabriel chose this place for teaching the Indians how to support themselves by ranching, rather than gleaning. They had to have abundant water for irrigation. They got it by diverting a portion of Mill Creek into a long transmission ditch — the "Zanja."

In 1820 the first crop was harvested. Some of the grain was stored in an adobe building located about 70 yards north of Mission Road. In modern times it was said that the spot in an orange grove could be found because the trees there were smaller.

95

The name Guachama—a small Indian settlement—entered into local history a decade earlier. According to Francisco Dumetz of Mission San Gabriel, he celebrated Mass there on May 20, 1810. It being the day of Saint Bernardine of Siena, Italy, he named it "San Bernardino."

George W. Beattie, our greatest research historian, was absolutely sure that the Guachamas of 1810 and 1820 were at the same location. This certainty is reflected in the text of the DAR plaque placed on the Mission Road monument in 1932.

But in 1976 Dick Thompson of San Bernardino persuaded his fellow members of the Native Sons of the Golden West that the Guachama visited by Padre Dumetz in 1810 was located on the diagonal road between the Orange Show and Colton. That, he said, is the place where the priest gave the name "San Bernardino." The Indian name was not precisely attached to one spot, he argued, and easily applied to the San Bernardino site in 1810 and the near-Redlands site in 1820.

Accordingly, the Native Sons established a monument which competes with the 1932 DAR monument in respect to the spot which Fr. Dumetz named "San Bernardino." If Beattie had been alive in 1976, he would have been enraged.

Both Beattie and Thompson, in their respective times, supported their opposing views with documentation and reasoning. All true-blue Redlanders, of course, will assume that Thompson was biased in favor of San Bernardino and that Beattie spoke the true word.

READING, 'RITING AND 'RITHMETIC

A bronze plate on a granite boulder at Church and Lugonia celebrates the beginning of public education in Redlands.

The first American settlers — the Mormon Colony at San Bernardino — started to have their children taught as soon as they had surrounded themselves with a stockade, safe from Indian attack. That was in 1851.

As early as 1857 the newly created county was divided into six school districts. As population increased in a district, it would be divided into two parts like the famous microscopic animal, the amoeba.

By 1877 there were enough people in the eastern San Bernardino Valley to warrant a new district. George W. Beattie, age 18, took the initiative.

In March he passed the teacher's examination.

He prepared and circulated a petition to create a new district out of a portion of Mission. This was granted, and the name "Lugonia," was adopted.

In order to establish average daily attendance on which public school money could be apportioned, the trustees decided to open school from mid-May to mid-June.

A small make-do structure was used on J. B. Glover's ranch at Texas and Pioneer. With Beattie as the teacher, that became the first school—but not the first schoolhouse.

Moving quickly, the trustees called a tax election to provide funds for a centrally located schoolhouse to be ready for use in the fall for regular classes. The proposal passed.

Who was the teacher? Why George W. Beattie, of course.

One historian recorded that he lasted only one month. That is not true. What confused the writer was this.

After two years, he swapped jobs with Mrs. C. E. Brink who taught in Colton but lived in the Lugonia District. She needed help. Her husband died in 1879. In 1881, her house burned down. She stopped teaching at the end of the year to devote herself to her four children. Beattie returned to Lugonia for two more years.

From this humble beginning in education, he advanced to become an important figure in San Bernardino County, in the state of California and in the Philippine Islands.

You might suppose, then, that the granite marker at Church and Lugonia has a double purpose—to memorialize him and the first schoolhouse. It does.

But Beattie created his own monument that will live as long as

Lugonia School Monument

intelligent people study the early history of this area. It is called *Heritage of the Valley — San Bernardino's First Century.* He researched it; his wife, Helen Pruitt Beattie, wrote it.

Beattie accomplished much in his book for two reasons.

First, he was close to the times of which he wrote. When he arrived in the valley, only 23 years had elapsed since the Mormon wag-on-train pioneers bought the Rancho San Bernardino land grant from the Lugo family. California had ceased to be Mexican territory only 26 years earlier. The mission era ended but 40 years earlier. During his young manhood he talked to many people who had made the history of which he would later write.

As an historian he was not a popularizer. He did not write a *Ramona.* Rather he was a patient, pedestrian researcher who went to the primary sources and unearthed documentary material that less persevering historians neglected. Thus *The Heritage,* not the stone, is the truly important and enduring Beattie monument.

CASA LOMA, LEGENDARY HOTEL

Through the intersection of Orange Street and Colton Avenue, thousands of motorists pass daily without noticing a low monument on the northeast corner. You can only read it while standing on the sidewalk. It says:

"Site of the Casa Loma Hotel — Redlands famous tourist hotel. Opened 1896. Became civic, cultural and social center. Presidents McKinley, Theodore Roosevelt and Taft spoke here.

"University of Redlands dormitory, 1939 until razed in 1955.

Casa Loma Hotel

[Plaque] placed by Arrowhead Chapter, Daughters of the American Revolution, 1963."

The ladies of the DAR are to be commended for marking an historic site. They are to be censured for casting in bronze a "fact" that is not true.

President William Howard Taft—unlike McKinley and TR —never set foot in the Casa Loma Hotel. He did not speak from the deck over the porte-cochere as they did.

Rather, upon arrival from San Bernardino, he was placed in the intersection of Colton and Orange. Standing up in the car, wearing a long duster, he spoke for about five minutes. Then he dashed off for a fast scenic tour of Redlands.

Although seemingly minor, the Taft error on the plaque hides an important point about our Presidential visitors. It was the railroad age that made it possible for Presidents to go touring about the broad USA, stopping at various points to be seen. They were driven in horse-drawn carriages.

The railroad era peaked here with TR's visit and, under the influence of the automobile, had begun to decline in Taft's time. In the future, Redlands would host no more Presidents.

GATES, FEW BUT FINE

From their palatial resort home, "The Breakers," at Newport, Rhode Island, the exclusive Vanderbilts shut out the world with a massive entrance gate.

The mansion builders of Redlands did not follow suit. If they built a gate—and few did—it was only an ornament.

You'll find the most interesting survivor from that period on West Crescent Avenue at the head of San Jacinto Street. On the knoll which overlooks that point, E. C. Sterling built his home, "La Casada," in 1897. Looking up the driveway you can probably see the red tile roof through a screen of trees.

That Sterling's fancy should run to masonry gates was natural

Sterling Gates

to him because he made his fortune in bricks. Or, more accurately, he made it from his patents on pressed brick manufactured in the U.S. Moreover, the gate was a handsome adornment to his Italian garden which climbed from Crescent Avenue to the house.

You will notice that there are four square pillars, the inward pair being the taller. On either side are gates for pedestrians. In the center is the carriage entrance. A crown-like grille spans the roadway—a point you should remember for what is to follow.

That the design came from the hand of a skilled architect is readily seen. The style is strictly classical. Ball and pedestal rise from a decorative molding, and terra cotta tiles adorn the faces.

Although Mr. and Mrs. Paul Hairgrove, present owners of "La Casada," sold the lots facing Crescent, they preserved the gate. It is crowded between houses but still proud.

If it were not for their energetic son, Doug Hairgrove, the story might be otherwise.

In 1985 a rookie driver of a city disposal truck failed to realize that after making a pickup he should leave the house by the service driveway. Instead, he went down the front drive with disastrous results. The pregnant truck was much too big. It virtually destroyed the gate.

A lesser man might have despaired, but Doug went about good-as-new restoration. He could get the iron work done in this area. A local mason knew how to rebuild the pillars. But the nearest place where the terra cotta parts could be reproduced was the Gladding McBean plant near Sacramento. Doug drove up there with the broken pieces and gave them to the moldmaker.

Doug was asked about the gates a thousand times before the terra cotta came and the job could be finished. He was mightily relieved when it was all over.

* * * * * *

You will find no gates where they might have been placed at the entrance to the mansion which Olivia and Caroline Stokes

Stokes Gate

built in 1908 on Mariposa Drive, well west of the Country Club.

They were women of enormous wealth. Philanthropy was their way of life. When their fancy turned to gates, it was for others — usually institutions — that they built. More often they gave much larger structures such as libraries, churches and college buildings.

In Redlands, though, it was not until one sister died that the other was moved to instruct her eastern architect to enhance the Alessandro Road entrance to Hillside Memorial Park. His design is classic, restrained and of manifest dignity.

The inscription on the gate reads: "In Loving Memory of Caroline Phelps Stokes. Born in New York, December 4, 1854. Died in Redlands, April 26, 1909."

Olivia was also moved by her love for her sister to give the land above the Stokes house, and below Sunset Drive, to the City. "Caroline Park" it's called.

The gate and the park should have squelched the old wives' tale that the ladies Stokes were scarcely on speaking terms and had separate quarters in their Redlands home. Gossip dies slowly.

Pleased with the Alessandro entrance to the cemetery, Miss Stokes provided in her will for an almost-duplicate set for the Sunset Drive entrance. The legend reads: "Bequeathed to the City of Redlands by Olivia Egleston Phelps Stokes, 1927." May the ladies Stokes rest in peace at Hillside Park in their adopted hometown.

FIVE WARS, ONE MONUMENT

A Redlander who goes sightseeing in any of the 13 original colonies is certain to take notice of many monuments to heroes of the American Revolution and of the Civil War. Most of them are sculptures. They range from the Minutemen at Concord to George Washington on horseback. In the South it is likely to be Robert E. Lee.

Returning to his hometown, the Redlander may feel that the City is impoverished. There are two Presidential busts — Lincoln in the Shrine and McKinley in Smiley Park by the Bowl. That's all. And no full-sized figures in bronze.

Moreover, until 1972 the City lacked a public monument of any kind to war veterans. Strangely, it was the most unpopular of the five wars in which the United States has been engaged since the founding of Redlands that did produce the Veterans Memorial on Redlands Boulevard at New York Street.

The Spanish-American War came first within the Redlands era. Company G of the National Guard entrained for San Francisco in May 1898 but remained at the Presidio there until the conflict was over. Two days before the "boys" returned in October, Private Harry F. Wallace died of spinal meningitis. On the sixteenth he was given the burial of a military hero in Hillside Cemetery. The tall, ornamental stone which stands over his grave is the only substitute Redlands has for a full-fledged monument to the Spanish-American War veterans.

If the community had had a tradition of public sculpture,

World War I would surely have spawned a monument. The war was a traumatic experience for those who served in it and for those "back home" in Redlands.

As things turned out the City Hall became a memorial of sorts.

Names of all Redlands veterans were printed in bold letters and arranged in columns on the upper walls of the entry corridor. Among the hundreds listed, those who died were easily identified by large gold stars.

In 1939 the building burned. The names were never restored in another place.

In 1926 an anonymous friend of the University of Redlands gave the funds to build the magnificent chapel. He said that it was to be a memorial but wasn't specific. A plaque is found in the foyer which honors UR Alumni who died in the military service of their country. There are 54 names in classes ranging from 1920 to 1966.

While the University is careful to call it "Memorial Chapel," the comunity is not inclined to so regard it. Townspeople think of it, mainly, as a concert and lecture hall. After all, the donor never said who the building memorializes.

During World War II, leaders in the Redlands post of the American Legion expected an explosive growth in their organization when the men and women in uniform returned to civilian life. There was a common expectation that a memorial would take the form of a palatial new clubhouse in a downtown location.

Surprisingly, the veterans of World War II did not exhibit the lively enthusiasm for comradeship that had made the Legion such a popular organization in the Twenties and Thirties. They seemed to be most interested in getting started on new chapters in their lives — in jobs, wives, children and homes.

No monument resulted from World War II, or from the Korean conflict which so quickly followed.

The prolonged war in Vietnam, with 50,000 American deaths and no victory in sight, created a sentiment that had not marked the earlier conflicts. Huge anti-war demonstrations were staged in various cities in the U.S. Student protests gave some campuses the appearance of battle zones. Opposition to the war mounted in Congress.

It seemed to many citizens that men and women serving in the armed forces in Vietnam were being denied the honor which was their just due. In Redlands this struck the most sensitive nerve among the Gold Star Mothers. They wanted a positive manifestation that their sons had not died in vain.

Approaching the Council with a proposal that some kind of monument be erected, they found their man in Charles DeMirjyn. He picked up the ball and kept running with it until completion of the Memorial on Redlands Boulevard.

It soon became a community project, furthered by veterans' organizations, service clubs, the City and firms in the construction industries. The advanced architectural class at San Bernardino Valley College held a design contest. The Gold Star Mothers selected the entry of Michael Coyazo, a graduate of Redlands High School. Robert Walker, RHS art student,

They asked not what their country could do for them.

Veterans Monument

designed the inscription, from President Kennedy's inaugural address: "They asked not what their country could do for them."

The monument was dedicated May 14, 1972.

Since there are no words beyond the inscription on the monument, the beholder is free to regard it as a memorial to all veterans of all wars, or specifically to Vietnam. In his dedication speech, however, Councilman DeMirjyn read the names of Redlands men who died in Vietnam. "It is to these 20 young men of our community that we dedicate this memorial," he said. "May there be no more."

A Sightseer's Tour of Sunset Drive

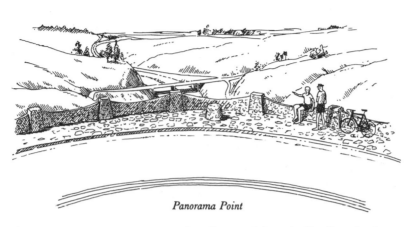

Panorama Point

ALTHOUGH THE AUTOMOBILE has been with us in Redlands since 1899, just driving around is still one of the most popular pastimes. As a route, Sunset Drive is the favorite. It's best to go clockwise — up Cajon, Garden and Hilton east to the drive; then go on around to the west end at former Smiley Heights.

Panorama Point is aptly named. On a clear day you can see in all directions. The highest peaks of Southern California — Baldy, Grayback and San Jacinto — raise their snowy heads in winter. Yucaipa Valley spreads to the east and the San Bernardino Valley to the north and west.

The observation platform on the point is built of beautiful brown rock which was hauled down from Bear Valley. It is a masterpiece of masonry from the hand of Elegio Benzor in 1936.

In the throat of Reservoir Canyon, just below the point, a grove of cottonwood trees, and water, attracted the Indians in their time. They left many stone artifacts about their campsite.

It is difficult to imagine the exciting chase up the narrow throat of the canyon that made history on May 30, 1851.

In pursuit were 40 Indians on horseback, armed only with bows and arrows. They were the defenders of the Lugo brothers Rancho San Bernardino.

Fleeing ahead of them, armed only with Colt revolvers, were the desperado, Red Irving, and his gang of 11 cutthroats. Galloping far enough ahead of the Indians, they were able to water their horses at the Sepulveda adobe about two miles farther east. Then they turned down Live Oak Canyon and crossed San Timoteo Creek. With Chief San Antonio's Indians closing in, the bad men turned into a narrow canyon with no outlet. They were massacred.

After the end of the Indian era, George D. Heron built his home in the cottonwood grove and added eucalyptus trees. There he bottled what he called "Mountain Crystal Spring Water" and delivered it by horse and wagon to many households in Redlands. His prospectus struck a romantic note in poetry:

> Bursting forth from the mountains bold
> Where Indians lived in days of old,
> Pure, cold and clear, from fountains deep,
> To freely drink, good health will keep.

Driving on around the Sunset loop you will notice on the highest point a water tank that it would have taken George Heron a lifetime to fill. The capacity is 3,000,000 gallons. It serves the highest elevation of the City of Redlands system, principally the nearby section of Sunset Drive.

Fashioned of steel, 91 feet in diameter and 62 feet high to the overflow line, the tank generates mixed feelings. One Redlander was so outraged by what he regarded as the marring of the skyline that he moved to Santa Barbara. Others like it as a local landmark that can be observed from the greatest distance. While coming down from Cajon Pass on the approach to San Bernardino, you can see it on any clear day.

Some old maps show the site of the tank as "Beacon Hill." American Airlines placed a light on a pole there in the pioneeer days of its route from Los Angeles to Atlanta. Later, the government established a chain of beacons through the San Gorgonio Pass and American took down the local one.

Just beyond the tank, Lanny Bruder built a doughnut-shaped, two-story house. No residential site commands a more panoramic view.

West of Hillside Memorial Park Sunset Drive follows the crest, opening a spendid view across San Timoteo Canyon. Strangely, the hills on the far side have no official name. The term "Badlands" applies only to a section of the range more to the east, that is, from the Moreno Grade (Redlands Boulevard) to the vicinity of Beaumont.

Up the bottom of the canyon runs the main line of the Southern Pacific, an historic route.

After completing the famous Central Pacific, which at San Francisco connects California to the East, the railroad builders came south. They were headed for New Orleans.

Construction progressed eastward from Los Angeles in stops and starts, passing through the Redlands area in 1877. By 1884 the links had been completed so that a traveler could go from here to Chicago, a common destination, with ease.

In the fall of 1884 a platform was placed in the canyon, below present-day Community Hospital. Residents of this area would be taken there by horse and buggy. They would flag and board a train.

During World War II the railroad became such a vital link in the supply line reaching out to the South Pacific that the system of central traffic control of the trains was started. This minimized the time one freight would have to stand on a siding waiting for an opposing train to pass.

The trains in San Timoteo Canyon are still under control from a center in Los Angeles, but the double track relieves the long delays of yesteryear.

You will see relatively few tank cars in the trains because an S.P. petroleum products line parallels the tracks.

Beyond the creek, the railroad and the orange groves you can see a huge, white disk. That is "Earth Station Redlands," built in

1983, as a ground link with General Telephone satellites in synchronous orbit over the Equator. Carrying data and telephone communication, it is hooked to the SPRINT system at Rialto by an underground "glass string" — the first major use of fibre optics in our immediate area.

In 1986 SPRINT laid a fibre optics line across the continent. Locally, it follows San Timoteo Canyon Road, buried and encased.

Raising your line of sight, you will see a dark rectangle at a higher elevation. That is a eucalyptus plantation that has been there since the memory of the oldest living Redlander.

In the latter nineteenth century, great stands of blue gums, native to Australia, were planted commercially in California for hardwood and oil. They proved to be of unsuitable quality. Extensive planting generally ended in the 1880s. The local grove has been swept by fire, again and again. New trees sprout after every conflagration, but each generation is smaller than the last.

Although you can't see it, the great San Jacinto fault passes just below the eucalyptus grove. From the west it has come out of the Reche Canyon ridge through a saddle. Going eastward, it crosses the crest and continues toward Hemet.

A carriage road up from San Timoteo Canyon road was built by the Smiley brothers, moved by their passion for scenic views. They acquired the knobs at the top of the hills and quickly communicated their enthusiasm to their adopted "home town." This is evidenced by introductory material in the Redlands City Directory for 1896:

"Tremont Park — On the low mountain range across San Timoteo Canyon stand three peaks. From them one can get an extensive view, including a vast area of mingled mountain and plain, comprising the sites of many villages and towns.

"It is impossible to describe this view in its wild and magnificent splendor of utter desolation, relieved here and there by the orchards and homes which the hand of man have brought into the midst of a parched and barren wilderness."

The same awe attracted many Redlanders, by car or on foot, until 1985 when the road was finally gated at San Timoteo Canyon Road. You may say to yourself that it doesn't matter because the smog would shut out the view, anyway. If so, that would reflect the popular notion that the air was crystal clear here until about 1940. It wasn't. Read one more paragraph of the 1896 description:

"The panorama is well worth seeing, especially on one of the *rare* days when every house on the distant plains stands out distinctly."

Hazy days were common before Henry Ford manufactured the first air-polluting Model T. Many tourists came here by train for the carriage drive over Smiley Heights and never saw the mountains.

The "Good Roads" Boosters

FASCINATED BY AUTOMOBILES, Redlanders bought them as fast as they could afford them after the turn of the century. They soon found, however, that cars can no more do without good roads than trains can do without good tracks.

Many fell victim to a virus that might be called "Good Road-itis." In Bill Moore's book, *Fun with Fritz,* you find John H. Fisher making the first trip from Redlands to Big Bear Lake in 1909 over an "impossible" route. In 1916 he led a caravan from Redlands to Salt Lake, preaching the gospel of good roads at each town along the way.

Some men were never cured. Like my own father, Paul W. Moore, *Facts* editor and publisher, they went to their graves with the bug.

In the final phase of "Good Road-itis" the obsession was the completion of a road to Bear Valley by Mentone, Mill Creek Canyon, Angelus Oaks, Barton Flats and Onyx Summit. At any meeting of the Chamber of Commerce it was almost impossible to avoid the subject.

As Columbus had envisioned the East Indies as the source of wealth for Spain, Redlands boosters long looked to the mountains as the source of business for the retail community. They were so steeped in this idea that large parties of volunteers would go up to Mill Creek Canyon and work with pick and shovel.

In the years just before the Great Depression, they were cheered when the U.S. Bureau of Public Roads built a ten-mile link from Angelus Oaks to the South Fork of the Santa Ana River. But the project stalled there.

In the late Thirties, the boosters promoted a horseback ride over the proposed link from the upper Santa Ana to Bear Valley. I am no horseman but I found myself pursuing our merciless leader, a cattleman. He would plunge into the barrancas, one after another, as if it were all in a day's work. Never sure if I would go over my horse's head, or slide off his tail, I did manage to stay with No. 1. The following day I was so stiff I could hardly stand up.

This field exercise failed to impress the Bureau of Public Roads. Not until World War II had run its course did they take up the project again. In 1961 the link where there had been no road at all was completed. At last, you could drive from Redlands to Bear Valley that way, instead of City Creek.

An appropriate Chamber of Commerce ceremony was held in the mountains, but none of the oldtimers had survived to attend.

Link by link the Bureau kept building new road until improvements were completed in 1978 for the entire length of Route 38 in the mountains.

It is strange how things often turn out.

What the Good Roads boosters had always envisioned was a road that would be driven for pleasure — not especially for utility. They would have been delighted in 1968 with the "Scenic Highway" designation given by the State Division of Highways.

They did not imagine, however, that Bear Valley would come to have a large resident population and that some of those people would commute to work in the valley towns. As congestion increased in Big Bear, itself, and on the route by Running Springs and City Creek, Route 38 became a popular alternative.

A Storm Over a Freeway

The story of the routing of Interstate 10 through Redlands is quite different. The passion for roads and more roads had cooled by the mid-1950s. The boosters had had their day.

What happened was this:

Under the leadership of Governor Earl Warren, the Legislature concluded that old-fashioned highways were obsolete. A new law opened with this statement: "It is declared essential to the future development of California to construct a statewide system of freeways."

This set in motion a continuing process by which most of the major routes would become freeways. Usually, it proved more practical to build on new alignments and to leave the existing roads for local use.

When engineers of the California Division of Highways studied possible alignments for a freeway in the Redlands area, two alternatives became apparent. The super-highway could bypass the city altogether in San Timoteo Canyon or it could cut through the town.

The response of the community was highly emotional with what seemed to be overwhelming opposition to a Redlands route. Underlying this position was a gut feeling that the super-highway would destroy the peace and tranquility of a town that is loved by thousands of residents. They liked the city the way it was. This monster of a road threatened to degrade the very qualities that make this a special place in which to live.

A public hearing arranged by the State filled the Fox Redlands Theatre. While the sincerity of the opponents is beyond question, a few were hysterical. "Our daughters will be raped under those freeway bridges," one mother shouted.

Supporters, on the other hand, understood the chairman of the California Highway Commission when he said in a local talk: "We are not just building freeways. We are building a master transportation system for the state of California."

It was transportation — railroad transportation — that made it possible to found and develop an orange-growing city before the turn of the century. Automobile and truck transportation were essential to the vitality of the city in the new era, supporters of the Redlands route believed.

The San Timoteo Canyon route was not preferred by the state for a couple of reasons. For one, it would deny freeway service to Redlands as well as to the ever-growing population of Yucaipa. For another, the freeway would have to be constructed all the way from about Loma Linda to Beaumont in a continuous series of contracts. That would not fit into the customary way of allocating funds for highway improvements.

In later years Dr. Lawrence Nelson, Redlands historian, offered a philosophical view. He said that the routing was not settled in the 1950s but in 1915. In the latter year a direct road from Redlands to Beaumont, through the future Calimesa, was completed. Once that alignment had been established, the state was destined to be committed to it forever — highway, freeway, or whatever.

Interstate 10 was opened all of the way from the Yucaipa Valley to the Colton Octopus on August 28, 1962.

During the period when the improvement was being so long delayed, Congress had adopted the Interstate Highway Act. This provided funding which made it possible to build three lanes in each direction instead of two.

From the hindsight of 1987, it can be said that the freeway changed Redlands into a commuter city. Every morning, Monday through Friday, the on-ramps are filled with the cars of people driving to work at locations which are within a radius of about 20 miles.

Barton Road

With the local freeway completed, the next modernization began on Barton Road. This was an old-style county highway — two lanes of blacktop which passed between orange groves for much of its length. From Redlands it was the route to Bryn Mawr, Loma Linda and Riverside.

In 1962 the road still made a zig-zag through the business and residential section of Loma Linda. With foresight, San Bernardino County established a bypass to the south by making a deep cut in a hill. The new road had four lanes.

Bryn Mawr had long been a hazard spot because Barton Road crossed the busy main line of the Southern Pacific railroad. By 1971 when money became available for construction, the County wanted to solve a second problem — floods on San Timoteo Creek. The solution was a long, high overpass riding above the wash and the tracks.

"But why didn't the bridge go straight ahead?" a modern observer might well ask. Because it was curved to avoid the packing houses by the S.P. tracks.

Pausing on the bridge today an oldtimer is likely to be saddened. There is little left of this village which at its peak had three packing houses, a passenger station, a telegraph office, a store, a school, a post office and a cluster of small houses.

The post office still exists, but in a new, off-road location. It is threatened by the steady expansion of Loma Linda.

Having started at the Riverside freeway in 1962, the improvements progressed eastward, at intervals, until Redlands was reached in 1979. The final job encountered a new phenomenon—the effective opposition of the Preservation Movement to "Progress."

From a traffic-flow standpoint it would have been best to eliminate the curve in Barton Road at the Alabama Street intersection. This realignment would have forced the moving or razing of a Queen Anne house. "Whoa," the Preservationists shouted. They—and they alone—saw a valuable artifact in this particular structure. Consequently the road was engineered to suit them, and never mind the lack of any plan for saving the house from the costly deterioration that inevitably comes with time.

Barton Road is today a busy thoroughfare—the most direct route from modern-day Loma Linda to Redlands. Thousands see in passing the two historical landmarks. Standing right by the road is the reconstructed Asistencia of Mission San Gabriel with its "trademark" bell tower. Just beyond it is the tall brick mansion built by Benjamin Barton in 1865.

In 1962 the present route included links with different names. When the road was modernized, County Supervisor Wesley Break of Bryn Mawr was able to establish one name through what are now four jurisdictions—Redlands, "the County," Loma Linda and Grand Terrace. He chose, of course, to honor Dr. Barton.

"Catch 22"—A Half-freeway

One more road problem remained. There came to be a need for an all-weather route from the Redlands side of the valley to the Highland side.

To the west, Norton AFB blocked off two historic routes, forcing traffic to the more easterly alignment of Alabama Street. Although the county widened that road, it could not afford to build a bridge over the Santa Ana river channel. Whenever the Alabama dip was flooded—and it often was in winter—the road had to be closed.

Ah, hah! But there was a solution in sight. The California Highway Commission adopted a route for a future freeway, east of Alabama Street, on the extended line of Tennessee. When built, it would provide the all-weather crossing.

Unfortunately, the state never could find the money to build the freeway. Catch 22! The County would not consider a bridge of its own because the State was going to build one, but the State wouldn't go ahead. The impasse was broken, after many years, by a local, political compromise.

By law certain State funds come down to local governments for road work. The projects on which they are to be spent, year-to-year, is decided by a commission composed of delegates from each jurisdiction. Councilman Chresten Knudsen of Redlands was able to make a deal. If money for the Tennessee Street Freeway were accumulated for several years, all the money would go to other designated projects in the following period.

This rocked the Tennessee project off dead center but in a peculiar way. Even with the additional money the State would put up, only a half-freeway could be financed initially.

Knudsen prudently saw that a half-loaf is better than none. The two-lane road would include the all-important bridge across the Santa Ana. Furthermore, the establishment of a half-freeway would eventually lead to a full freeway.

In two projects, Route 30 was built in 1983 and 1984 from Interstate 10 in Redlands to Fifth Street on the north side of the river. Current State scheduling contemplates that by 1992 Route 30 will be linked to the so-called "North-side Freeway" in San Bernardino and to Route 330, the route from Highland Avenue to Running Springs by way of City Creek Canyon.

These remarks would not be complete without saying that the original, grand plan was for a Foothill Boulevard routing of a new freeway. It would have reached from San Bernardino through Pasadena and all of the foothill towns and terminated in Redlands at I-10. Political obstacles have frustrated the original concept.

3

HISTORY A LA CARTE

The Saga of City Hall

PATROLLING AT 1:47 A.M. on February 3, 1939, Police Officer Joe Hook looked up Orange Street and saw flames.

It was City Hall, at Cajon and Vine.

He raced three blocks to the fire station. Four engines rolled. All hands — regulars and reserves — converged on the conflagration.

They were too late. Saving the large, three-story brick building was impossible. Flames were already licking up the open stairway and penetrating the roof.

They did save the Presbyterian Church, just across Vine Street, but somehow its ultimate destiny seemed fixed in the stars. On the night of June 28–29, 1967, it burned to the ground. So did the Methodist Church at the Lord's Corner, a block south.

When daylight came on February 3, Fire Chief Perrin Trowbridge said: "Ever since I have been in Redlands, I have expected this building to burn down. There were no fire walls, no safeguards. It was built to burn."

The genesis of that building dated to 1887. In that year Redlands pioneers contracted YMCA fever and held an organizational meeting. (Incorporation of the City was a year off.)

By 1892 they had expanded their aspirations beyond their first quarters on State Street. They would build a temple that would express their zeal for things Christian.

With crusading enthusiasm they raised $25,000. The Quaker Smiley brothers, of course, were in on it. Frank E. Brown, co-founder of Redlands, chipped in a generous donation of $1,000.

They chose a site at the center of the city, a decision of enduring importance. This we shall see as the story progresses.

There was no setback. The "Y" was flush to the sidewalk on Cajon and flush to the sidewalk on Vine. The vacant ground on the north side would, in effect, become sacred when the Smiley brothers included it in their four-block-long park.

Lee Burton, the architect, gave them what they expected — an imposing brick structure, voluminous as a major church and looking back to the culture of Europe for its themes. There was, for example, a two-story turret with a conical roof overhanging the street corner. And the main entrance was through a broad arched opening in the Romanesque Revival style.

Old City Hall

The founders, though, were not fools. They had no notion that all of the building would be needed for the activities of the YMCA. Rather, they provided much space that would be rented. The income would be needed.

One feature was an upstairs auditorium. In that day, the "Y" was the frequent sponsor of lectures, musicales, ice cream socials and prayer meetings.

Alas, in creating Redlands as "the Athens of the West," the YMCA enthusiasts went too far. Their pretentious temple was just too much financially. They had to sell it.

Looking for a permanent home for City Government, the Council was happy to acquire the building for $25,000. In addition to providing plenty of office space, the police station could be accommodated in small quarters which faced Vine Street.

There is, however, a natural law of community affairs that has guided Redlands for generations. It is this: After 40 years a public building will seem to be obsolete. Authorities will replace it if they can.

This law caught up with City Hall in the 1930s. Its implications were to remain unfinished business on the Redlands agenda for nearly a decade.

In 1931 Isaac Ford — always the visionary with dreams of an evermore beautiful Redlands — was seeing more than a new City Hall. An esplanade would start in Smiley Park by City Hall, wind by the Library and end at a grand auditorium just north of the Bowl. The esplanade died aborning. The auditorium dream never does, recurring from time to time with variations.

In 1933, the Council decided the time had come to raze the 41-year-old building. The new structure would not be so crowded on the site because it would be set back from Vine. However, this meant that it would move north into Smiley Park. Ruth Drake spiked that idea. As the niece of A. K. and A. H. Smiley and the daughter of Daniel Smiley, she was the surviving champion of their ideals.

The Smileys, she explained, were acutely aware of the common tendency of public authorities to place buildings in existing parks instead of acquiring other sites. In the document setting forth the conditions of their gift of the downtown park, they had explicitly forbidden invasion of the land for non-park purposes.

In 1935 members of the Council thought they saw the way out of the site trap. A Hall of Justice would be constructed on Fifth Street north of what is now called Redlands Boulevard. In it would be the police station, the court, and a judge's chamber.

Freed of the police station, a new City Hall on the same site would meet the needs of the municipality. A one-story building would suffice because it would have a full basement.

What made this two-building plan seem economically feasible was the availability of unlimited labor, cost-free to the City. The federally-financed Works Progress Administration would provide all of the workmen needed. The City would be responsible for purchasing the steel, cement, wire, lumber and so on.

About the proposed style there was no uproar. It was to be "Spanish Mission."

Engaged to design both buildings was a "hometown boy" in whom the community took justifiable pride. He was Paul

Ulmer, a graduate of Redlands High School, the University of Redlands and the Harvard School of Architecture.

He executed the plans for the Hall of Justice. The WPA carried them out. But the Council found that the City Hall could not be financed simultaneously with the Hall of Justice under restrictions placed on it by the federal rules.

Mr. Ulmer could not wait. He left town for greener architectural pastures in Indiana. That is not the end of the story of his services to the City, as we shall see.

In 1936 Mayor Will Fowler proposed a bond election in a speech to fellow members of the Rotary Club. Not to be left out of the spotlight, Councilman Mancha Bruggemeyer took up the theme in his typically florid style of oratory at a Knights of the Round Table luncheon.

With Mr. Ulmer gone, Architect DeWitt Mitcham of San Bernardino was engaged to draw the plans. The building was to have a full basement. A Council Chamber would be on the second floor.

With the Depression obstinately lingering on, the People were in no mood for a bond election. Many orange growers were mortgaged up to their necks, businessmen struggled to survive and hundreds of men and women were unemployed.

But dang the Depression! Somehow Redlands just had to have that new City Hall. In 1937 the Council designated Maurice Clapp, one of its most aggressive members, to pick up the ball and run with it. He did. By November 15 he was saying that demolition of the one-time YMCA building would begin on December 1. The plans for which the City had paid Mitcham would be used.

His cantankerous political foe, Theodore Krumm, dashed into court to get a restraining order. It was improper, he declared, to use water department reserve funds to partially finance the construction.

In 1938, stalled once again, the Council could do nothing more than wistfully review the plans and hopes of earlier years.

Then, in 1939, came the fire. No roadblocks remained—

political or financial. The Council was free, at last, to build a new City Hall. The taxpayers would have to give their consent.

The Councilmen's motto should have been: "Make haste slowly." Instead, they were lured by the availability of work-relief labor if they acted swiftly. The members knew what they wanted—a fireproof, earthquake-proof, functional building. Architect DeWitt Mitcham had committed this design to blueprints in 1936. With a few updates to accommodate ideas that had come up in the past three years, his plans would be all right.

Mitcham, however, believed that his work would have to be done all over again. He bid $3,400 for the job. William Allen of Los Angeles was not pessimistic. He undertook the project for $2,400 and moved rapidly. Within five weeks the *Redlands Daily Facts* would be able to publish a picture of his rendering of the proposed building.

A public storm broke. Never mind that the building was functional, that it filled the order: a Council chamber and utility space in the basement, offices on the main floor, and a flat-floored auditorium on the upper floor.

To conservative Redlands eyes, Allen's design was "too modernistic." The facade would have a band of bas relief pictures at porch level but the massive expanse of concrete above was windowless. On the north and south sides of the building the windows would be separated by plain, narrow members giving a strongly vertical composition.

Many locals were horrified by Allen's copper roof—not a single covering for the whole building but four perimeter slopes. Each one would be about 12 feet wide. (Most of the roofing would be flat and invisible from ground level.)

And sin-of-sins in the Redlands book, there was no "Spanish influence." Allen tried to explain the rationale of his design, but his message fell on deaf ears. Knowing when he was licked, he surrendered to local taste and promised the ornamentation that was desired. He died hard, though, about that roof. He felt strongly that copper sheathing was correct. It would come to have a beautiful green patina. But he gave them red tile.

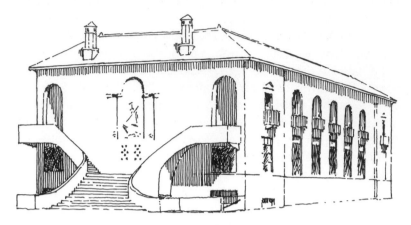

"New" City Hall
(rear view)

This was a typical Redlands exercise. What mattered was appearance. It should surprise no one that it was the composite "Beautification Committee" that dictated the ornamentation of the building. This ad hoc group was made up of two members each from the Planning Commission, the Beautification Committee of the Contemporary Club and the Beautification Committee of the Chamber of Commerce.

The ladies of the Contemporary Club, especially, demonstrated power to override the City Council — to have the last say. Those women were strong-minded and strong-willed. They were never known to take "No" for an answer.

WPA officials, in their original dealing with the Council, had bargained for immediate construction. The change of architectural plans resulted in many months of delay. Major construction began late in 1939 and continued through 1940.

In retrospect, it is interesting to consider the thinking of 1939. What this review demonstrates is that we are all prisoners of the age in which we were brought up and in which we are living.

Within 10 years, Downtown Redlands would begin to suffer for lack of off-street parking. Within 20 years, the scatteration of business and services would be underway. Eventually the City would have to acquire the immense, underground parking garage just across Cajon Street to accommodate vehicles of employees of the government, itself.

Yet, in 1939 parking was not an evident concern of anyone.

As to the auditorium on the upper floor, it was considered possible that it would have to be used for occasional large meetings. Otherwise, the City, itself, would have no need for this public facility.

But by 1956, the City was so cramped for space that it became necessary to convert the auditorium into partitioned offices. Never again would the Assistance League be able to hold its elegant Charity Ball there as it did in April 1941.

Why wasn't the growth of Our Town, and therefore of our municipal government, expected in 1939? Because Redlands was paralyzed by the Great Depression. The population in 1930 had been 14,177, and the 1940 census would show no significant change. It took World War II to stimulate new growth, beginning in 1942.

Today the Municipal government overflows City Hall to quarters in the Redlands Plaza, just across Cajon Street, which the City owns.

An inspection of City Hall, inside and out, is worth your time.

Walk clear around it and you will notice "The Beautification Committee's" red tile roof, the "Spanish influence."

The massive facade, disliked by the critics of Allen's design, is punctuated with three windows. That's better.

Five broad windows on the Vine Street and Smiley Park sides seem to rise to two stories to round tops. Each is broken at the second story by a balcony enclosed by ornamental metal work.

You are likely, for the first time, to notice the bas relief panels on the sides, near the front.

Ironically, the most majestic view is from the back. The stairway rises briefly from ground level and divides into two imposing sections. Between them is a bas relief which in 1939 was said to be of a ship sailing around the Horn. You will laugh when you notice that the sails are supplemented by nine oarsmen on the visible side of the vessel. Cape Horn? Really?

The irony is that the grand staircase, which seems to be an important entrance, leads only to locked doors. Originally they served the auditorium. Now, the offices which occupy the second floor are entered only from the interior front stairs.

Going into City Hall by the front door — not the park door — you will see that the WPA did not give Redlands a Plain Jane interior. Instead, artists were allowed to do their thing, especially in designing ornamental tile patterns. A huge compass, in several colors, dominates the floor of the foyer. It incorporates citrus and mission themes.

On the second floor you will find panels of inlaid wood over the doors leading into the offices.

In the basement? Yes, the artists went down there, too.

The mahogany panelled Council Chamber is long gone. The Council meets at Safety Hall, Brookside at Eureka.

During sessions in the old chamber, an odd thing would happen. The Air Force was then operating a huge cargo airplane called "The Globemaster." If one flew over City Hall, the basement windows resonated to the beat of the four engines in the sky.

You may be puzzled by the plaque placed on the floor of the porch by the Native Sons of the Golden West. It declares that City Hall is dedicated to "Truth, Liberty and Toleration."

I do recall a marathon search there, during the 1950s, for the truth of what was going on in the troubled police department. Otherwise, I am wondering about the relevance of the lofty motto.

There was aggressive intolerance by the American Civil Liberties Union in 1986 for a small cross as one of the various symbols on the City seal. "Liberty"? She's a lady in New York Harbor, isn't she?

Before you finish your visit to City Hall, take note of the lovely park. Where a driveway occupied the ground in the Smiley brothers' day, a nicely curving walk now passes from Cajon to

Japanese Garden and Peace Pole, City Hall Park

Vine. Just beyond the walk a small Japanese garden was laid out, a token of Redlands' Sister-City relationship with Hino.

The small, rectangular fountain is dry. What a pity! It memorializes our long-time city engineer, George Hinckley, who "brought us water." The fawn, though, is nice. Millard Sheets, the noted artist, designed it.

Fawn on Hinckley Fountain, City Hall Park

Standing behind the building, you would never guess that it extends over ground where men used to pitch horseshoes in the days of the first City hall. And only oldtimers remember the adjacent, rustic structure where a man could always find someone with whom to play checkers or cards.

Now there are no intrusions into the beauty of the landscaping. From the green lawn rise clumps of trees — crape myrtles that blossom in July, pines that raise a tall wall of evergreen, and very tall Mexican Fan Palms.

The Smiley brothers would love it.

Oh, yes! You thought I was going to forget to finish the Paul Ulmer story didn't you? No, I was saving him for last.

In 1936 he ran out of time and did not design the City Hall proposed by Mayor Fowler but never built. Later, he returned to Redlands.

He was the architect of Safety Hall, a building that did get built. It is unique in Redlands and a monument to his skill.

U. of R. Comes of Age

Chapel, University of Redlands

THERE'S A FAMILIAR SAYING that "the native should never return." He will be disappointed. So many sights have changed that his cherished memories would seem to be about a different place.

This is true of Redlands in many ways, with one major exception—the University of Redlands campus.

There he will stand on the steps of the imposing Administration Building, looking up at the tall columns. The portico is as timeless as the architecture of ancient Greece and Rome that inspired it.

Looking northward, he will see rows of large oaks marching toward the Memorial Chapel. That grand structure appears today as it did in 1929 when it was dedicated.

Yes, the native is home, at last.

But wait! His first impressions will change as he tours the grounds.

He will find that science and engineering buildings have been wrapped around the side of "Ad Hill," facing Sylvan Park. To the south, the campus has jumped the trickling Zanja with a theater and a speech building.

Returning to the hill, and then going down to walk around the Quad, he will pass dormitories with unfamiliar names.

By now he is ready to discover what may appear as a new and secondary campus just to the east of the Quad buildings.

Across a broad lawn he will see a set of three fine buildings which were erected for the former Johnston College. They stand out, naked and bold, with no landscaping to veil them.

Even more impressive, and grouped with them, is the large Armacost Library, modern in style.

Upon reflection, the returning native will gain an inkling of the evolution of the campus.

All the construction has been done in waves. The Founders

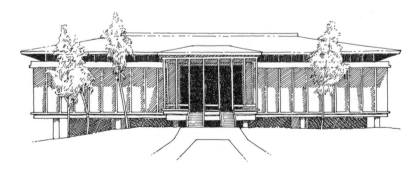

Armacost Library, University of Redlands

were able to erect the Administration Building, one dormitory and the mansion for President Fields. That was about all. For a decade it seemed as if the so-called "university" had been stillborn.

But beginning in 1921, and continuing through that decade, the ailing college was born again with almost continuous construction. By the time the Depression gripped the campus, Business Manager George Cortner had managed to provide the basic buildings the U. of R. needed — dormitories, classrooms, library, gymnasium and chapel.

Then, for 20 lean years, the school was paralyzed by the hard times of the 1930s and by the War era of the 1940s.

As fate would have it, the presidency was open in 1945. The Trustees found their man in Dr. George H. Armacost. For 25 years he would place his stamp upon the University, through and through. This would include doubling the number of buildings to 40 and almost completing the plant.

It is no wonder that when a Redlander travels afar he encounters strangers who know of the University but not of the city. The sprawling town, comprising many different developments over the span of a century, may appear to have "just growed," like Topsy. But the campus retains that sense of plan and order established by Jasper Newton Field and architect Norman Marsh when they placed the main building on Administration Hill and designated an open Quadrangle for the placement of future structures.

Moreover, the University is a model for the Preservation Movement which is gathering momentum in the city at large. Under President Douglas Moore, the school sold $7,500,000 in bonds to finance the heavy overhaul of buildings that were deteriorating, and the modernization of others, wherever necessary.

Redlanders are destined to love the University for the glorious link to the past that it will long provide.

While the view from Ad Hill may carry the viewer back to 1929, the school has evolved and changed so much that it is not the same institution. This is true of how it is organized, of the students it serves, of student life and of the constituencies that support the institution.

Although the organizational chart may not show it that way, there are two Universities of Redlands today. One is the familiar college with about 1,200 undergraduates. Most of them have come directly from high school, they live in dormitories and all student life is campus centered.

The one exception is the U. of R. in Salzburg, Austria. About 35 students in each of the two annual semesters have enrolled there since 1960. When not engaged in conventional study, they travel in Europe. This is an eye-opening experience which quickens their interest in foreign languages, European history and world affairs.

Quite different in nature is the other "half" of the University of Redlands. It is dedicated to adult education. About 1,600 fully employed men and women are the students. They live and work in towns and cities of such populous counties as San Bernardino, San Diego, Orange and Los Angeles.

The technical name for it is "University of Redlands – Whitehead Center." "Whitehead" is apt because Alfred North Whitehead of Cambridge and Harvard Universities espoused a philosophy of lifelong learning.

But the word "Center" is likely to fool you. Instruction is widely decentralized, currently being given in 41 locations.

Classes are organized in Southern California wherever 15 or more students would like to enroll. They may attend classes at regional centers — the Redlands campus, Irvine in Orange County, San Diego, central Los Angeles or Encino in the San Fernando Valley. Or the location may be a manufacturing plant such as Rockwell International at L.A. Airport.

Whitehead was launched with a pilot program in 1972. It took off like a rocket. The experiment indicated that hundreds of men and women hunger for sound, college training to further themselves in their careers. Most of them are able and willing to pay the cost of bringing the classes to places that are convenient for them.

While providing a valuable service to the students is the primary goal of Whitehead, it also provides an additional source of tuition income for the always hard-pressed U. of R. budget.

Of the 1,200 undergraduates who live on campus, about 70 are enrolled in the Johnston Center for Individualized Learning at this writing (1987). The program is explained to prospective students in a brochure which says:

"The graduation contract is the cornerstone of the educational process at Johnston. Instead of bending your academic goals to the institution's requirements, you negotiate the individual terms under which you will graduate from college.

"The process begins with conversations with your academic advisor. Together you'll plan an ideal personalized curriculum, taking into account such factors as your proposed concentration, post-college plans and the modes of learning that are best for you. Then you'll measure your list of ideas and dreams against Johnston Center's guidelines for graduation contracts."

After a stormy shakedown, Johnston appears to have found its permanent niche.

It all began in 1965 when planning started for an experimental college within the University of Redlands structure. President Armacost and the Trustees had before them the example of the Claremont Colleges, 35 miles to the west. Like Redlands, this complex started as a single, liberal arts school—Pomona College. Beginning in 1926, new colleges were founded until the total reached six. Each has its own campus, faculty, student body, board of trustees and endowment. They share a library and some special facilities.

The academic reputation, the solvency and the architectural accomplishments of Claremont were persuasive.

In 1966, Trustee Dwayne Orton persuaded James Graham Johnston to make a founding and naming grant. The two men had been colleagues in IBM, and Johnston had made a fortune in the company.

The Trustees hired Dr. Pressley McCoy as the first Chancellor of Johnston College. Three first-rate buildings were constructed for the new school. Further space was provided on the ground floor of the Armacost Library.

Johnston College opened September 2, 1969, with 89 men and 92 women students. Important things started to go wrong immediately. In a dramatic confrontation before the students and faculty, McCoy declared: "We have the right to determine our own social rules." Armacost vehemently replied: "Pres, you don't and you never did." Social rules? Well, the Johnstonians insisted on such things as a "right" to keep dogs and cats in the dormitories.

Then Jeanne T. Friedman, an alleged Communist, appeared on the campus on the day of her arrest on two felony counts at Stanford University. McCoy hired her as a faculty member. The conservative people of Redlands were incensed. Johnston College lost local support and never regained it.

Whether the original concept of Johnston College could have succeeded is problematical. My own opinion is that it could not. From a financial viewpoint, Dr. Armacost had seen the cluster college plan as a means of broadening the supporting constituency of the University. Instead, Johnston was undercapitalized from the start, did not attract the number of expected contributors and became an intolerable burden on the University's budget.

Moreover, the timing was impossible.

In 1964, the Free Speech Movement at the University of California, Berkeley, triggered a student rebellion against authority. This became nationwide and was exacerbated by student hostility to the Vietnam War. It became almost inevitable that the first Johnston College student body would include a number of dissidents who would make it impossible to achieve the consensus which was crucial.

Individualized learning was not a new plan in 1969. Stanford had offered it since the 1920s, with few takers. But Johnston had the misfortune to be born in a turbulent time that was not of its own making.

To work, the school had to be revamped, redirected and

brought into the fold. It also had to survive — which it has — until the return of fair weather on college campuses.

Now housed in Bekins Hall, formerly a women's dormitory, Johnston has low visibility.

While the controversial years of Johnston make a lively chapter, it is the transformation of the Old U. of R. into the New U. of R. that is the broader story.

The character of the University was shaped at the outset by its parent, the Baptist denomination. With a strong emphasis on religion, it is not surprising that students were required to attend chapel every morning, Monday through Friday, like it or not.

Furthermore, the Trustees swallowed the doctrine of *In Loco Parentis* whole. The University would act in the place of parents, assuming full responsibility for the lives of the students.

The Baptists of that period had an extremely straight-laced view of social behavior. Students were forbidden to play cards or to smoke. That they would be allowed to drink was absolutely unthinkable. The repeal of Prohibition in 1933 made no difference.

And then there was dancing. That, too, was unacceptable. The policy became explicit in the first academic year, 1909–10, and was seemingly cast in concrete forever.

While the ban on cigarettes and alcohol was understandable to the townspeople, the ban on dancing was not. Indeed, this was identified as one of the important social graces by two of the most prestigious ladies in the community. They were Mrs. J. A. Kimberly and her daughter, Mrs. Elbert W. Shirk. For years they personally sponsored and chaperoned dances for high school-age boys and girls each fortnight at the women's clubhouse.

More than any single thing about the University, the no-dancing policy marked the campus as a Baptist preserve, separate and different from the community at large. Redlands was not the happy hunting ground it should have been for Presidents in search of philanthropists who would finance new buildings and bolster the endowment.

It was not until World War II that the outdated bonds were broken.

After Pearl Harbor the student body began to shrink at an alarming rate as the men either volunteered for military service or were drafted. To keep afloat, the U. of R. had to have more students.

In 1943 a contract was signed with the government for the housing, feeding and educating of Navy and Marine officer candidates.

A Navy V-12 unit arrived on July 1, 1943, 631 men strong. Bolstered by 110 civilian men and 473 women, the total enrollment of 1,214 students in 1943–44 was the greatest ever.

Officer candiates would be a familiar sight on campus until October, 1945, when the program ended.

Since military men were not required to attend chapel, this was the first break in a 34-year-old policy. However, when World War II was over and the V-12 unit departed, compulsory chapel was destined to continue until the student militancy of the 1960s. The administration fought a rear guard action, retreating step by step from 1965 until 1968 when Convocations were made voluntary. Attendance thereafter, on Thursdays, rarely exceeded 100 students.

As to the bans on smoking and card playing, John Scott Davenport, who was one of the Marines, wrote an irreverent recollection in 1985 for "The Redlands Report." In it he remarked parenthetically:

"Mind you, there was always at least one poker game going on during off-duty hours in whatever dormitory Marines were occupying. Pipes, cigars, and cigarettes abounded. There was a beer route — into the back of Grossmont Hall after dark — established in the fifth month."

Having set the stage with those remarks, he went on to Topic Number 1 — Dancing. Let him tell it:

"Denied an official opportunity to celebrate on a balmy New Year's Eve in 1943, the Marines pulled out all stops. For starters they wired the Memorial Chapel with loudspeakers connected to a record player, then passed the word to key coeds. That evening, between hourly musters, there was a gala dance on the

University's holy of holies. Glenn Miller's 'Jersey Bounce' could be heard all over Redlands and half way to Colton. . . . Someone finally turned off the record player after midnight. All of Redlands was surely aroused, but no gendarmes appeared."

Two months later the Navy held a proper dance in the Commons. The Trustees now had a graceful out. They could discard a policy which had become quaint. In 1945 they did.

Let it be said that while Davenport wrote of the hell-raising Marines with amusement, he did not fail to add: "Before World War II came to an abrupt halt, Redlands Marines were in combat. They fought on Palaus, at Saipan, Tinian, Iwo Jima and Okinawa. . . . A number were recalled to command platoons in the icy hell of Korea . . . a few went on to Vietnam." Similar words could be said on behalf of the Navy men.

While the V-12 unit helped to break student life out of the Victorian mold in which it had been locked, nationwide social trends would bring further change.

Instead of being the very strict "parent" of earlier years, the University would give students more and more responsibility for deciding how late they could stay out, week nights and weekends. Fraternities and sororities, which had never had quarters of their own, were permitted to build houses near the Zanja. In 1987 there is one sorority house and there are four fraternity houses. They are for social use, not for residence.

The traditional practice of housing students by sex has virtually collapsed. Coed dormitories are in. Peek into the lobby of a residence hall and you will invariably see both men and women.

Now there are eight coed dormitories, two for women and one for men.

Another change is the participation of women in intercollegiate athletics. Some of these sports are basketball, tennis, soccer, volleyball, swimming and diving, and track and field.

Now, leaving student life, consider the evolution of the University into a broadly oriented, liberal arts school. Some of the threads of this story are unique to the U. of R., but most of them

are common to the American experience in the era of
1945–1987.

When World War II was over, many veterans enrolled under
the GI Bill of Rights and lived in a "Veterans Village" on campus. They were purposeful and more mature than traditional
undergraduates. Faculty members found themselves challenged
in a manner they welcomed.

Elsewhere in the United States, the GI Bill made it financially
possible for many men to earn their Ph.D. degrees. The local
consequence was that there was a larger pool of highly qualified
candidates to select from when hiring new professors.

Conditions since World War II have attracted professors to
the United States. A number of them have enriched the U. of R.
faculty.

Paul Pisk came from Vienna and headed the music department. Henry Dittmar, German by birth and education, British
by later experience, and American by choice, stimulated student interest in World Affairs. The welcome mat was kept out
through the years bringing professors from different lands. One
of them at this time is Angel Aparicio-Laurencio, a Cuban, who
teaches Spanish.

In 1946 Congress adopted the Fulbright Act providing for the
exchange of professors between the United States and many
other countries. This made it possible for a faculty member to
study abroad for a year. Many, and in different departments,
seized the opportunity. Erwin Ruff, in music, chose Vienna.
Jay Krantz, in science, selected Pakistan. Ward Miller, in
English, went first to Finland and then to Jordan for an encore.
Robert Morlan, in political science, was fascinated by Amster-
dam and returned there for further study and writing.

At home, various professors found an opportunity open to
them that had not existed before the war. They could get grants
for research from the new national agencies in science and
humanities. In science departments, where there were four or
five professors, the tendency was for each to become a specialist.

In the mid-1950s the jet age began. Europe, which had been

nearly two weeks away by train and boat, could be reached in 12 hours by air. The days of parochial teachers and students were over. The world had become everybody's oyster.

As the new University of Redlands grew in stature, it was able to attract public figures of great interest. Among them have been the peripatetic Eleanor Roosevelt and the immensely popular poets, Robert Frost and Carl Sandburg.

Politicians began to take interest in the University. Campaigning for Vice President and President of the United States, both Republican and Democratic candidates came to the campus in 1960. Two years later, as a candidate for Governor of California, Richard Nixon returned to the school he had first known as a member of the Whittier College debating team.

Throughout the period since World War II, the University has gradually evolved from a predominantly Baptist institution into one which values diversity in faculty, student body and trustees. Consider:

—Dr. Douglas Moore, the seventh president of the University, was the first non-Baptist. He was a Methodist.

—Historically, the Board of Trustees always had members who were Baptist ministers. They were influential in policy matters. Today, there are no clergymen on the Board.

And here is the blockbuster: only eight percent of the students this year are Baptists. They are one component of the 50 percent who are Protestants. Catholics, once a miniscule segment, now comprise 37 percent of the student body.

The school is really interdenominational. It continues to have a strong Christian emphasis in policy and practice. That is a distinguishing characteristic and the reason why many parents want their sons and daughters to come here.

From an off-campus viewpoint, the most remarkable turnabout is the warm relationship between town and gown.

Some of President Armacost's predecessors tried hard to remove the chill. One of them was Clarence H. Thurber. He became highly controversial and resigned in 1936 under pressure from "narrow-minded Baptists," many townspeople thought. They gave a testimonial dinner for him with 182 citizens signing an appropriate scroll.

Elam J. Anderson, a popular man on the platform, made so many public relations speeches that the Trustees had to blow the whistle on him. (He died after a brief term in office.)

It was left to President Armacost, who arrived in 1945, to successfully heal the breach. He was much aided by the general feeling of good will in the community that persisted in the wake of the War. Consider:

—In 1947, the organization of support groups began. First, The Fellows—friends of the University who make annual contributions to the budget.

—In 1948 the first paid director of the Alumni Association was hired. This gave unprecedented vitality to U. of R. graduates living in Redlands as a supporting force.

—The large banquet hall added to the Commons was given strong Redlands identity by naming it the "Casa Loma Room." The name was taken from the large frame and board building at the northeast corner of Orange and Colton which was, at first, the major tourist hotel in town, and, at last, a dormitory for U. of R. women. So many Redlands events are held in the "Casa Loma Room," it seems to townspeople that the community actually owns it.

—When high school football games became immensely popular, larger facilities were needed. The new stadium was financed jointly by the University, the school district and the City. This is also the location of the great patriotic event of the year in Redlands—the Fourth of July celebration.

—President and Mrs. (Verda) Armacost threw themselves into the life of the community so thoroughly that they won the hearts of everybody.

Although Dr. Armacost has not been President since 1975, the community and the university seem to be as one. Presidents Eugene Dawson and Douglas Moore carried on where he left off. In recent years, enthusiasm for the University has been organized under the banner of "Town and Gown."

If there is one event that especially instills love for the University in the hearts of townspeople, it is the Feast of Lights. Staged annually in the Chapel since 1947, this glorious celebration of Christmas in song and pageantry is profoundly moving for the 6,000 people who attend the four yearly performances. They come away feeling that they have been in touch with the very soul of the University.

Sports – Games – and Fitness

ERADICATING ORANGE GROVES in their path and sweeping over the land, housing tracts have changed the landscape of Redlands so much that an oldtimer would hardly recognize the place.

But there is one new element in the landscape he would notice before anything else — people in motion. If you drive about town any time from dawn to dusk, you can't fail to see people who are walking, jogging or playing a ball game.

There are many reasons — and I will mention a few — but the underlying one is that our people are anxious to keep physically fit. They are health conscious as never before. It has become an article of faith that regular exercise is necessary. You have to get up and stir around to feel good and to live as long as you would like.

I drive about three miles to work every morning. In that brief journey I never see fewer than three walkers. Some days there are 10. Man-and-wife couples are the most common. Most of them have gray hair.

Joggers? Anywhere from three to six. What would astound any oldtimer is the women. Women never ran in public until 10 or 15 years ago. Now they are out on the streets and sidewalks everywhere. They have stamina and run for miles.

What is more surprising is the mass passion for sports activities — especially youth sports. At this time soccer is almost a madness. Perhaps as many as 3,000 people are involved as players and as supporting adults. On Saturdays the large field at Moore Junior High swarms with activity all day.

For most adults, the modern eagerness for physical activity is quite a change from pre-World War II Redlands. One oldtimer put it this way:

"You worked hard at your job. If you had any spare time at home you mowed your lawn and took care of your yard. Now people are paying to have their places taken care of. The men who are hired to do the work usually have a truck or pickup, as well as lawnmowers and tools. You see a lot of them."

Also, many a Redlander had a citrus grove as well as a job, or a store, or a profession. Take the late Bill Barlow, for one. He cut hair six days a week at Harvey Phillips' elegant, marble-panelled barber shop. He lived in a house in his five-acre grapefruit grove. On Sundays he pruned, irrigated, trapped gophers, and oiled to suppress weeds.

The five-day week has become standard for most men and women who work. They are at leisure on Saturdays and Sundays. Many escape from the town over the weekend for a variety of activities. In winter, skiing is a big thing. The desert attracts countless Redlanders in their vans, campers and trailers. They have numerous off-road "Jeeps," motorcycles and all-terrain vehicles.

The building of dams and reservoirs to quench the enormous thirst of Southern California has put numerous lakes within automobile reach of Redlands. Lake Perris is only a 30-minute drive. There you can find friends with catamarans, power boats, water skis and fishing poles.

Distant though it is from here, the Colorado River exerts a magnetic attraction. It would have been unthinkable to go there in summer before World War II. Now you'll discover, in casual conversations, that many folks have mobile homes parked there and will spend a week by and on the water.

Whether at home or afield, the television set and its influence have become inescapable. The man or woman who watches tennis matches might say: "Maybe I would like that game. I think I'll try it."

A young person cannot realize that broadcast television did not become popular until around 1948. Nor had the riches of TV created the opportunity for the champions of golf, tennis, football or baseball to become very wealthy. In this new era, several Redlands men have gone on from high school and college to professional football — careers that were undreamed of a few decades earlier.

In looking back over both eras of Redlands — the first half century and the second — it is apparent that almost no sport has enjoyed constant popularity. Horseback riding, a craze in the late '40s, is now at low ebb. Competitive bicycle riding was a madness in the late 1890s, quickly died and did not revive until the 1980s.

Why?

Periods of depressions and prosperity have a lot to do with these ups and downs. In the 1930s, most orange growers were almost broke. Only a few were enthusiastic about riding. But when prosperity returned a decade later, you should have seen the costly Tennessee Walking Horses on our bridle trails.

For another, great wars interrupt the normal course of life. A diversion that was popular before may not be afterward. Night badminton was played on numerous home courts late in the Depression. After Pearl Harbor, when Japanese raids on the West Coast were feared, the Army ordered blackouts. This was a blow to badminton; the game died out and has never come back.

Enthusiasms shift. When the automobile was introduced in Redlands (1899), men who had been crazy about bicycles transferred their enthusiasm to cars. The factory-made skateboard did not appear until after World War II. Every boy seemed to own one. The popularity ebbed, for a time, and has returned to full tide. On nearly any afternoon you can see kids coasting on streets, sidewalks and sloped pavements of every kind.

In wondering why various sports become popular, you have to look beyond the games themselves. One wise observer put it this way:

"People are gregarious. We like to do things together.

"People like to talk. Men do, but women more so. On the court they may talk as much as they play. At the Little League game, my wife will miss the start of the home-run play because she is talking to her friend sitting next to her.

"Women like to show off. They get those tennis outfits where everything matches, and they sure look sharp. Don't you think that increases the popularity of tennis?

"Parents, too, I think often live their lives through their children. They like to have their kids have the fun they missed. Mothers are forever carting their kids all over Redlands. They may not have watched a baseball game in their lives before, but they become fans.

"Whether the players are the kids or the women themselves, games get women out of the house. It gives them something to do."

A philosopher might wonder if people are as much attracted to sports for sociability as for the games themselves. Homes have become very private places with little neighborliness.

One man said to me today: "I haven't seen the doctor who lives next door to me in a month. The fellow on the other side and I had a little chat about three weeks ago."

Whatever the sport, it brings people together. Maybe that is the ultimate explanation of the sports phenomenon.

Now let's take a look, in detail, at sports, games and fitness.

GOLF

Imported from Scotland, the game dates here to 1897 when the Redlands Country Club was founded. The early "greens" were sanded and oiled. In 1927 a full, 18-hole course with grass greens opened, and it has remained basically the same ever since.

The club made a considerable investment in land, in sprinkler systems and in maintenance equipment to establish the fine course. But the Depression began here in 1930 and the deeply indebted club went broke. A bank sold the property to J. "Mack" Johnson in 1941. The clubhouse, built in 1901, burned down in 1942.

Years of adversity followed, but a group of the faithful managed to work out the financial problems until, finally, Redlands Country Club again owned the 18 holes.

Fires wouldn't quit. A new clubhouse, built in 1948, burned in 1961. A bigger and finer building was opened in 1963. It is equipped with fire-control sprinklers.

Golf enjoys great popularity at this time, although Redlanders who do not belong to the Country Club often have difficulty getting on the crowded courses elsewhere in this region.

TENNIS

Like golf, this is an old game in Redlands – in fact, even older. Reading a diary kept by Frank P. Morrison, I found that he played tennis here in 1882 at the home of his future father-in-law, Dr. J. D. B. Stillman. The court was somewhere on the present campus of the University of Redlands.

There is poetic justice in the location. Today, there are 10 courts at the University – more than in any other location in the city.

Furthermore, a club was organized here so early that it supplied the first president of the Southern California Tennis Association, John W. Wilson.

As a social game, tennis continued to have popularity through the 1920s, a prosperous era in which a number of home courts were built. The Depression, however, almost killed tennis except for the high school and the University.

In 1962 tennis was still so dead in Redlands that I couldn't arrange a game, as an act of hospitality, for a new resident. The men I telephoned were playing at Perris Hill in San Bernardino or in Palm Springs.

Then came a surprising turn of events.

In 1963 Redlanders poured their enthusiasm into the Diamond Jubilee of the founding of the city government. One event was a tennis tournament, directed by Coach Jim Verdieck of the University of Redlands. So much interest was sparked that a proposal to form a club found immediate favor. It was off and running. By January 1964 the Redlands Racquet Club was a vigorous, incorporated organization. At the first annual meeting Dr. James Fallows was elected president.

This was no flash in the pan. The popularity of tennis in Redlands was not only revived but broadened and deepened. In 1967 Ted Burke proposed to build a club near the Mariposa School, about a mile east of the Country Club. In December he was formally joined in the venture by 10 limited partners.

Called the Redlands Swim and Tennis Club, the facility includes two swimming pools and seven cement tennis courts. Two grass courts can be set up — the only ones in Redlands.

School courts are popular: five at Cope, six at Clement and seven at the high school. The Country Club has a pair as does the Community Center owned by the City.

Overton Pratt, a tennis enthusiast during all of his adult life, put a court on the roof of the large sporting-goods store which Pratt Brothers built at Citrus and Church.

Even more novel is the set of seven courts at Ford Park. The City did not include them in the plans for the new domestic-water reservoir which was to be built there. Vehement members of the Racquet Club objected to this omission. The Council agreed that the flat, concrete deck over the water was an excellent place for tennis.

To my knowledge, no census of home tennis courts has been taken, but I would guess the number may be around 40. Perhaps the total within the city, including all kinds, approaches 100. Quite a few are lighted for night play.

BASEBALL

"Play ball."

With that familiar cry, dozens of boys raced out to four diamonds, warmed up and began to play baseball.

The date was June 18, 1961. The occasion was the formal dedication of Redlands Community Field on San Bernardino Avenue at Church Street.

This was far, far from the beginning of the game in Our Town. As early as 1888–89, Redlanders fielded a team which won a league championship. They played right downtown on a field that is now within the Mall.

Within a decade, the Redlands Bicycle Club would include a baseball diamond in its seven-acre development on Colton at Herald. The game continued its popularity in the public schools.

But it was the development of a program in which there were leagues, classified by age for boys from 8 through 16, that would attract hundreds of players.

The basic enthusiasm for baseball inevitably involved the City. A grapefruit grove at Texas and Colton was bought, cleared and developed. However, the California Division of Highways needed part of the property for a section of the new freeway. The $72,000 the state paid, with additional money contributed by citizens, made it possible to buy the northside land.

The Colton and Texas diamond was informally known as "the Little League field," but somehow the name did not seem transferable. Leaders fussed over the new facility. Should it be named for someone in Baseball for Boys? No, that wouldn't do. So many people had played prominent parts that no individual could be singled out and honored.

As all-male sports gave way to participation by women, Baseball for Boys became Baseball for Youth. However, the girls have not taken over the game. If 900 youths signed up in the past season, the girls numbered about 50.

The genius of baseball as a mass participation sport lies in its adaptability to any age group or level of skill. In Redlands they start out in T-Ball, just old enough for batting and fielding, but not yet ready for pitching. Long after their Baseball for Youth years, men still enjoy the game in the less strenuous version known as "slow pitch."

While Community Field continues as the major center of baseball, the game naturally finds other fields including the YMCA and those on various school grounds.

The term "Community" could well extend beyond the field to

reflect the fact that many men and women, organizations, and businesses support the activity. Thousands of hours of volunteer service are contributed every year. If the champions of 1888–89 could somehow return, they would exclaim: "Bravo! You've kept the faith."

FOOTBALL

1849. That's a magic date in California history—"The Gold Rush."

1949. That's the year in which Redlands discovered football as an athletic game and as a spectator sport.

In the past, football had been in the doldrums. The Redlands High School Terriers took it for granted they would never win the Citrus Belt League Championship—not against such big schools as Riverside, Pomona, and San Bernardino. Except for parents, few Redlands adults attended the games.

There was a bit more interest in the University of Redlands Bulldogs, much of it from local alumni.

In the summer of 1949, the tide suddenly turned. The Los Angeles Rams rolled into town, established their annual training camp on the University campus and began daily workouts.

Big League football! Famous names! Sports glamour! Redlands was enthralled. The red carpet rolled out. The Rams players, in turn, were friendly with the locals—yes, girls too.

Redlanders became Rams fans and made countless trips to Los Angeles to see the team play. Their cup "runneth over" in 1951 when L.A. clipped Cleveland, 30-28, in the Coliseum to win the championship.

The Rams were here for 13 years. The big event was always the annual scrimmage. As a benefit for UR scholarships, this netted $14,000.

The year of 1949 also brought Coach Ralph "Buck" Weaver to Redlands High School. He started a revolution by teaching a simple lesson. The Terriers could win—win against the big schools in the CBL. The town went crazy. At a 2:00 P.M. rally on the steps of the gym, the students didn't really know how to cheer; they had to be taught. A spontaneous parade through downtown followed. Everyone was hyped up for the victory that ensued.

It's an odd thing about sports. Nobody can do it until somebody does it. Then other people can do it. In the mile run, four minutes stood as a barrier through which no man could pass. In 1954, Roger Bannister of Britain broke the tape at 3:59.4. That mark was successively lowered 15 times in the next 25 years.

Buck Weaver broke the 4-minute-mile barrier for the Terriers. Their success continued under other coaches. The climax came in 1961, when a team coached by Frank Serrao, defeated El Rancho, 14-6, in the L.A. Coliseum, to win the Southern Section, California Interscholastic Federation title for large schools.

With football fever rapidly becoming an epidemic, the adult fans—including the fathers of players—organized the vigorous Benchwarmers. They became the prototype for fans who coalesce to boost their favorite sport—tennis, swimming or whatever.

By 1968 high school football had such a large constituency in the community that it was possible to build a new stadium on Brockton Avenue. This was made possible by a lease-purchase agreement with the University in which tax monies were made available through the City and the school district. The debt was paid off rapidly.

One of the reasons RHS has such a devoted following is that large high schools play against each other. Redlands meets some powerhouses from Orange and Los Angeles counties. The day cannot be far off when ever-growing enrollment will force the school district to establish a second high school. RHS may continue to field strong teams, but they will probably play lesser rivals.

SOCCER

The rest of the world has long known that soccer is the best game of its kind. Unquestionably it is the most popular international sport, played in 140 countries. It has been an Olympic event since 1900. Unlike baseball's erroneously called "World Series," soccer's "World Cup" competition is truly that.

At last Redlands is catching up with the rest of the world. Started here in the 1970s for youth, soccer has made phenomenal gains in the last five years.

Under the pattern established by the American Youth Soccer Organization, players and parents have found a game with which they are happy and comfortable. Cost is held to a minimum. Every child gets to play. There is no arguing with the umpire. The action in the game is continuous.

As in baseball, soccer is organized so the kids play in the ability group where they fit. Girls can run and kick and have as much fun as the boys.

The broad turf fields that serve public schools, readily adapt to soccer. It is simply astonishing to see how many games can be simultaneously played at, say, Moore Junior High, on a Saturday and how long through the day they play.

SWIMMING

If you could have taken a sightseeing ride in an airplane over Redlands in 1947, the thing you would probably have said is: "My goodness! I knew there were a lot of orange groves, but not that many!"

Take a spin today and your comment is likely to be: "Swimming pools! I never imagined we have so many in Redlands."

The first-time aerial sightseer is always surprised because, on the ground, he hasn't seen them. Nearly all are behind houses and hidden from the street. But from the air they are conspicuous. They look like blue tiles and are geometric.

How did it happen, this building of pools by the hundreds, by the thousands?

By the 1950s the developers of housing tracts created lots that would accommodate both a home and a pool. Savings and loan associations and banks made it easy to finance pools. Builders learned how to install a pool by new construction technology and by the adaptation of available materials.

In the hot summer climate of Redlands, a swimming pool is a joy for everyone—your own kids, the neighbors' kids and the parents. It is natural to want one. By personal values of yesteryear, a pool was a luxury. Today, it is almost a necessity for many families.

As swimming pools became more and more popular, the City Plunge in Sylvan Park declined in favor. The City Council allowed the dressing rooms and the pool itself to deteriorate badly. Officials began to take smog alerts too seriously and would chase kids out of the Plunge in the early afternoon. Fewer and fewer returned in the following days. Finally, the Council had to decide whether to close the Plunge or to spend a lot of money on renovation or new construction. That was the end. The concrete was bulldozed out, and the hole was filled in.

That is not, however, the whole of the story.

In 1922, when the City built the Plunge, recreational swimming was the big thing. The pool was a place to have fun with one's friends—splashing, diving, swimming on the surface, swimming underwater and talking, talking, talking.

By 1946 a general trend in youth sports was overtaking swimming. For those who were serious about athletics, competition was the thing. Redlands High School discovered in the water what it was learning on the football field. The Terriers could win championships in their League and in three ability groups.

This trend was strengthened by the Redlands Swim Team—a group of boosters devoted to the training and development of competitive swimmers. In the mid-'60s the School Trustees, responding to pressure, consented to the building of two pools on the high school campus. Sylvan Plunge — dedicated to recreational swimming — had lost its constituency.

Although he lived in Redlands for only a few years, one beneficiary of the interest in competitive swiming was Robin Backhaus. He was a star of the Terrier team, and graduated from RHS in 1971. While in Redlands he was able to turn to Coach Walt Anderson to help him perfect the butterfly.

In 1972 he was a student at the University of Washington, but Redlands was still his home town. Going to Munich as a member of the U.S. Olympic team, he won a bronze medal in the 200-meter butterfly. He hoped, of course, to win a gold, but that was not to be. His teammate, Mark Spitz, was just too fast.

The best was yet to come. In the 1973 World Championship, he won the gold medal in the 200-meter butterfly.

BOWLING

While such sports as tennis have seen periods of popularity and of decline, one game seems to keep sailing along on an even keel. That is lawn bowling. It was here in the first half-century of local history, and the Redlands Lawn Bowling Club continues to be a devoted band.

Perhaps more than any other Redlands game, it lends itself to visitations by teams from other countries — Canada, for one, and Australia for another. The matches are played on the home greens which are located on University Street, in the corner of Sylvan Park.

Before World War II, the companion sport of indoor bowling was located on Orange Street near the present freeway. Unfortunately, its reputation was not good. A bowling alley was regarded more like a pool hall than like a genteel bowling green. The post-war years would bring a drastic change.

What spurred a revolution was the invention of automatic pin-setting machines and the televising of contests. The looked-down-upon stepchild of pre-war times grew into the most popular indoor participation sport in the United States.

Redlands is not an island. What sweeps the nation inevitably washes over us.

Local promoters incorporated Empire Bowl, sold shares in it and built a 24-lane "Brunswick house" on West Colton Avenue. It opened in 1960.

As in other cities, bowling had instant appeal. In the typical fashion of participation sports, leagues promptly developed, stratified by age, ability and sex. Competition begins with boys and girls, ages 8-14. It becomes unisex during the day, in housewife leagues, and mixed sex with couples playing against couples in the evening.

Bowling has also become a popular family sport. An innovation of recent years makes it easier for anyone — child or adult — to get started in the game. That is automatic scoring. "The computer" does it for you.

PRIVATE ENTERPRISES

Three recreations have attracted investors — skating, shooting and racquetball.

Roller skating found a downtown home at Vine and Fifth in what had been the Mission Garage for years. The rink was a great improvement over cement sidewalks. When that property was wanted for the Redlands Plaza development, the rink moved to a new building which is just east of Alabama Street and just south of the Freeway.

Empire Skate, in common with other sport/recreation businesses, has regional drawing power. In this case, about from Yucaipa to Fontana.

During the Twentieth Century, Redlands shooting ranges have been located in various places. Eventually, the Santa Ana wash proved to be the most convenient and suitable.

The Winchester Trap and Skeet Range was established in

1964, just west of Orange Street and at the base of the bluff. Gerald and Sue Eubanks have owned and operated it since 1980.

Trapshooting resembles the once-popular sport of quail hunting in the brushlands south of Sunset Drive. The clay pigeon "flies" away from the shooter, rather low, but at random angles.

Skeet shooting is much more complicated with the clay pigeons simulating the flights of various game birds, including ducks. The most impressive challenge comes when two high targets fly towards each other. Shades of Buffalo Bill! It takes a sure shot to shatter one clay disk and instantly knock the other one to pieces.

On the far side of the wash, on Orange Street, the Inland Fish and Game Club also has skeet and trap ranges, but the big thing there is pistol and rifle shooting.

The racquetball building on Colton Avenue attracts men and women who like a fast, hard game. The ball is slightly larger and softer than a handball and is struck with a shorthandled racket. There are eight courts, each being like a four-sided box with high walls.

SPORTS SPECTACULARS

In the 1980s Redlanders developed a penchant for annual races which bring a lot of competitors to town.

It began in 1984 with the Run Through Redlands. By 1987 the field included 2,020 men and women, competing in eight events. The toughest is the half-marathon, 13.1 miles, starting Downtown and going around much of Sunset Drive Loop.

While attending a conference in the east on the ways of promoting Downtown, Mayor Carole Beswick took a strong fancy to bicycle racing. The first Redlands Bicycle Classic, in what became an annual series, was held on Memorial Day 1985. No one could live in Redlands without an awareness of this spectacular because it is spread over four days and the courses pass through residential districts for miles.

Redlands had been a poor town for serious bicyclists since the turn of the century. Suddenly, interest revived and big crowds lined the streets for the most glamorous events. What gave the Classic prestige was the participation by Olympic riders in the Critereum (40 miles and a 1.2-mile course) and the 80-mile finale, much of it on Sunset Drive. In 1986 Davis Phinney was the star, but Raul Alcala was only 15 seconds behind him in the final event. Erich Heiden, the great Olympic ice skater, also added luster to the Classic.

Bringing girls from all over the country were the YMCA National Gymnastics Championships in June, 1987. The main events were staged in the Y's Roy Coble Gymnasium and the University of Redlands Gym.

This overview of sports has covered a variety of topics. In conclusion, it should be noted that the YMCA has become to athletics what Barnum, Bailey & Ringling Brothers has to the circus world. It's the major center for physical fitness, games and recreational sports in town.

For years, the Great Y Circus lived up to its billing as a thrilling show. It ended in 1986 because liability insurance had become too expensive.

The so-called Young "Men's" Christian Association has, in fact, become a family institution. Largely through sports, it helps people grow in spirit and improve their physical condition. It aims to—and does—strengthen families through common activities.

Doctors on the Move

ARRIVING IN 1887 in the dusty new village called "Redlands," Dr. M. W. Hill rented office space on the second floor of the Union Bank building. That placed him at Orange and State, the intersection that would become the very center of town.

For nearly 80 years "Downtown" would be a powerful magnet, attracting doctors, druggists and hospitals. Should I also mention undertakers?

Then the Redlands Community Hospital became a magnet of equal power. A second center developed on Terracina Boulevard. As of 1987 the division is about equal. Forty-three M.D.s have offices in the old district and 42 in the new.

Our mobile medicos provide a fascinating study in the dynamics of Redlands. They have moved from one location to another in response to ever-changing influences. They are one element that makes this a living city and will continue to be so for generations.

Although early doctors were attracted to the central business district, they soon began to scatter up Cajon Street for several blocks. In the manner of the day, quite a few built homes in which they had their offices. This was a practical arrangement, especially in view of the fact that they had evening as well as daytime office hours. If they needed to make a house call, they could walk a few blocks to a livery stable and rent a horse and carriage.

With the advent of the automobile, it became practical for doctors to live at a distance from town and most of them chose to do so. The final holdout was Dr. David C. Mock. In 1921 he bought the practice and combination office-home of Dr. John L. Avey. There he saw his patients until his retirement in 1955.

In 1904 a group of doctors built a two-story hospital on Nordina Street at Clark. This was within one to three blocks of most offices and tended to stabilize the medical geography of the city. Several new offices were created in this zone by converting small houses into offices or, in one case, into a laboratory.

The 1920s brought prosperity to what the Chamber of Commerce called "The Navel Orange Center of the World." Cadillacs were "in." Model-T Fords were "out." Redlands was ready for an upgrading of medical facilities.

Should the town have something better than the Nordina Street Hospital? E. M. Cope, a leading citizen, thought so. In 1927, he contributed his 17-acre orange grove on Terracina Boulevard at Fern Avenue as the site for a Community Hospital. This single act was destined to have a powerful influence on the medical geography of Redlands – but not for almost 40 years.

The one-story hospital, with red tile roof in the Spanish manner, was built during 1928 and opened March 18, 1929. Seven months later the stock market crashed. The ensuing Great Depression, followed by World War II, froze the facility at its original size for 20 years.

Although the Nordina Street Hospital would close within a year, ending its magnetic power, a fine new professional building was constructed in 1928. The Medical Arts Building at Vine Street and Sixth, brought the greatest concentration of doctors to the Central Business District that the city would ever see.

Medical Arts – brand new and planned for physicians from the ground up – was a smashing success. One by one, doctors deserted their old locations. By 1936, and perhaps earlier, the twin wings were "full up." The occupants included one dentist, a lab, the City Health Officer, and 11 physicians.

If up-and-coming younger doctors wanted high-quality offices, who would build them? They would. In 1937, Dr. Charles J. "Pat" Clock, four years in practice here; age 37. Then, in 1940, Dr. Meredith G. Beaver, nine years in practice here; age 41.

Both located on Cajon Street, as close to Downtown as available real estate permitted. In the case of Dr. Beaver, this proved to be a landmark decision.

In 1940 he might have had the radical idea of abandoning Central Redlands and locating his modest professional building near the Community Hospital. But the time was not ripe. Fern Avenue at Cajon best suited the convenience of himself and his physician-tenants. It also suited the patients. Indeed, the remote location of the hospital created difficulties in an era when few nurses had their own cars, and two-car families were the exception. Shouldn't the hospital have been on a site nearer to "town"? Many wondered about that at the time.

World War II closed a chapter in the medical geography of Redlands and set the stage for the next one:

—With the establishment of Norton AFB in 1942, a permanent increase began in the population of the city, Mentone and Yucaipa. Redlands would be a place of opportunity for more doctors.

—The war sucked off younger physicians leaving only 13 to take care of 14,000 Redlanders. It was an exhausting time. The older ones would be ready to retire within the next decade.

—The post-war period created conditions that favored the construction of half-a-dozen "professional buildings" of modest size. Dr. C. T. Halburg led off, adjacent to Medical Arts. He returned to the favored style of the 1920s, California Spanish. Then a new march began, up from "town" on Cajon Street, just as if the Nordina Hospital magnet were still there. Dr. Philip Loge teed off with a two-doctor building in a refreshing new style.

There is an affinity of dentists for doctors, and the "teeth men" became neighbors of the medicos — either in professional buildings or free-standing buildings of their own.

—Dr. Beaver was in the Army during the war years. Upon his return, he and three others with whom he had served in the military formed the nucleus for the team of diversified physicians that became the Beaver Medical Clinic. They were so successful that today the staff is comprised of 31 doctors and a large supporting organization.

In founding the clinic, the four doctors gradually took over all the space in Dr. Beaver's attractive building. But they were destined to have growing pains for years, one major expansion of the plant following another until the building would extend for a block on Fern from Cajon to Fourth.

During this period of growth, Beaver and associates were, like Hamlet, torn by a root question—"to stay or not to stay," in the same location. They felt the same tug that doctors were feeling elsewhere in California—to move closer to the hospitals where they practiced. Consider, for a moment, what was happening at Redlands Community.

After 20 years in the same facilities, the new era began. On June 25, 1950, the MacDonald Maternity Wing opened. On June 29, 1958, a double celebration was held for the Moseley and Radiology Wings. On December 4, 1966, the tower was dedicated. The hospital had grown from 40 to 195 beds.

While the patient capacity of the hospital was growing so much, a second factor was getting to the doctors. The hospital was the central location for more and more high tech equipment for diagnosis and treatment. It was convenient to be near the hospital.

Like the indecisive Hamlet, the clinic group decided that the time had come to abandon the historic medical district, close to town, and relocate near the hospital. A large site for a new building with plenty of parking was purchased at Terracina and Olive. But the agonizing continued. The new site would make it difficult for various patients who walked to the clinic. The Beaverites reversed their decision, sold the distant site, and completed the Fern Avenue plant.

It remained for someone else to break away from town and make the mile-and-a-half leap to Terracina. Who would have the courage? A newcomer, freed from the tyranny of the past? No, not at all—quite the contrary. He was Dr. Howard A. Hill. Look at the family tree:

As you will recall, it was Dr. M. W. Hill—first generation— who launched his practice in the bank building at Orange and State in 1887. Dr. Howard G. Hill—second generation—eventually joined him and then succeeded him. Howard's sons, Harold and Howard, became the third generation of Hill doctors in Redlands. All four had offices in Downtown, or within a few blocks of it.

When Dr. Howard A. Hill felt the time had come, he was joined by Dr. Richard J. Wilson. They—and further associates —bought land directly across the boulevard from the Community Hospital, and in 1965 built the Terracina Professional Building. In 1987 it accommodates radiology, a lab, physical therapy and 13 doctors. Oh, yes, and a pharmacy.

Until the postwar period, you went to a drug store to fill a prescription. That would be Downtown, or at Winn's on Colton at Orange.

When Dr. Beaver persuaded veteran druggist Wilson Spoor to locate a pharmacy in the clinic, a new trend began. Terracina Professional, distant from all drug stores, had to have a pharmacy for the convenience of the patients—and it did.

A secondary effect of this trend was to weaken the grip of Downtown on drug stores. They were destined to abandon the soda fountains and lunch counters which made them social gathering places, especially at noon. Today, only Winn's still has a counter.

Terracina Professional was also a trend-setter in another way. The project included not only the medical building but a convalescent hospital on an adjoining site. Terracina Convalescent Hospital, as it is called, was followed by Brookside Convalescent Hospital on Terracina and Brookside. Are there more to come?

Once Terracina Professional was built, medical siting shifted from town to hospital. The small Redlands Orthopaedic Center came next. Then, a whopper!

Investors led by Dr. Tom Harkness and Dr. Gerald Rutten acquired the site at Terracina and Olive which the Beaver Clinic had bought and sold and built the $3,500,000 Redlands Medical Center. It was occupied in December 1979. The offices are located in a square surrounding an elaborate garden. In 1987 it housed 26 doctors as well as supporting facilities, and other tenants.

Redlanders had become conditioned to thinking big about medical facilities, but the $45,000,000 reconstruction of Community Hospital was a breath-taker. Planning began in 1978; dedication came in 1985. The 195-bed hospital included not only the five-story triangle wing, but a great elaboration of all the facilities that comprise a super-modern hospital. A broad range of specialized programs — undreamed of at the founding in 1927 — are offered. Although located in Redlands, the hospital serves a broad geographical area.

Just when it seemed that the hospital was the final word, a surprising counter-development occurred. A group of physicians decided that one-day surgery could be offered more economically and more efficiently in a new and specialized facility. They built the Inland Surgical Center on Laurel Avenue, within a block of the hospital.

While "Doctors on the Move" has been an all-Redlands story up to this point, Loma Linda cannot be left out.

In 1961 the Seventh-Day Adventists organized Loma Linda University to consolidate medical, nursing and paramedical programs. In 1967 the seven-story University Medical Center was completed. Like a lighthouse on the shore, this became a beacon which would attract doctors with extremely specialized skills. They would be served by rapidly evolving, high-technology equipment which is very expensive.

This was destined to regionalize medicine to a certain extent. It was economically impossible for each hospital to have every variety of costly equipment. Redlanders began to take it for granted they would go to University Medical Center for skills and services not available at the Community Hospital.

At the same time, community feeling became more regionalized. Loma Linda was no longer an Adventist enclave — a world apart from Redlands. Numerous Loma Linda specialists bought or built fine homes here and joined in the spirit of our town.

Wherever people live they now have a strong interest in good health. It unites them in common humanity.

Redlands, Host to Presidents

ROSES, ROSES, ROSES. They picked them by the basketful, they picked them by the bushel.

While fog still hung over Redlands on the next morning, May 8, 1901, they scattered them for blocks on Orange Street.

They said it with flowers: "Welcome, William McKinley, President of the United States." Leaving his special train at 10 o'clock, the distinguished visitor rode in a splendid carriage, drawn by four milk-white horses, to the Casa Loma Hotel, beginning a day Redlanders would never forget.

Every history book about Our Town celebrates this most glorious day. But none of them goes on to say that the story of visits by men who have been President begins with a shout and ends with a whisper. It ravels off until nothing is left but trivia. So, let's put it into context and order.

Why, in the first place, did William McKinley come to Redlands, a new city with only 6,000, or so, inhabitants?

The answer is found in the development of the western railroads. Although the transcontinental rails were joined at Promontory Point in 1869, it took 20 more years to extend lines within California, north and south, east and west. This network made it possible for incumbent Presidents to tour about California in hope of strengthening themselves with the voters.

Benjamin Harrison, elected in 1888, found time for railroad touring. Although his itinerary took him to mainline cities such as San Bernardino, Riverside and Corona, he did not switch to the Santa Fe branch line to Redlands.

It was McKinley who would come here first — on the Southern Pacific and over a full-gauge track that was only seven years old.

While Redlanders liked to believe that the President came

here for the sole reason that they had created the wonder city of Southern California, there must have been more to it than that.

For one, there is the Machiavellian adage of politics: "Reward your friends and punish your enemies." McKinley did have friends in Our Town.

In the election of 1896 which made him President, he was favored in Redlands 571 to 201 over William Jennings Bryan.

In the rematch election of 1900, the Republican ratio improved further: 732 to McKinley, 237 for Bryan.

Whooping it up for McKinley were several prominent citizens. Among them were Republican "fat cats" who joyously put their money where their mouths were. One of them was A. G. Hubbard, the mining millionaire. He invited all Redlanders to be his guests on a train trip to a political rally in San Bernardino.

Was it coincidental, then, that Hubbard rode in the carriage of honor following the President with Mrs. McKinley and Mrs. Henry Gage, wife of the Governor of California?

There would be one more great Presidential visit to Redlands, almost two years later to the day. McKinley had been assassinated. Theodore Roosevelt became President. Taking a leaf from his predecessor, TR went railroad touring. Thanks to his influential friend, A. K. Smiley, he included Our Town for a carriage tour and a speech.

All went well until the finale. Roosevelt complained to John H. Fisher, head of the mounted honor guard, that in each place he visited, the locals were late getting him back to his special train. Fisher said: "Don't worry. I'll get you there on time."

Nonetheless, the carriage tour fell behind schedule. Fisher was concerned. Riding beside the carriage, he said: "Mr. President. Do I have your permission to tell your driver to gallop the horses?" The leader of the former Rough Riders did not hesitate to say "yes."

Redlanders standing on the curbs, from Prospect Park to town, complained that they did not get a very good look at Roosevelt. But TR did get to the Santa Fe station on schedule.

There would again be complaints of Presidential speeding

down Cajon Street, but this time the visitor would be in an automobile. He was William Howard Taft.

Poor fellow. October 12, 1909, was a terribly exhausting day.
Like Harrison, McKinley and Roosevelt, he opted for railroad
touring, but away from the train he moved locally by automobile, not by carriage.

His managers scheduled a 12-hour day. It began in Los
Angeles, continued by rail to San Bernardino, came onward to
Redlands by car, went on to Riverside's Mission Inn for dinner
and, at last, back to the train.

For Redlands, this was not a re-run of the glorious McKinley
and Roosevelt visits. Rather, after taking Taft up and down the
streets of San Bernardino, they brought him to Redlands in an
open car. At Colton and Orange streets he did not go into the
Casa Loma Hotel; he did not speak from the deck over the
porte-cochere. Instead, he stood up in his car and gave a short
homily for the assembled school children.

As they dashed him up to Smiley Heights, the engine of the
car became so hot the driver had to pause to cool the radiator.
Never mind. The locals showed no mercy. He sped on to Prospect Park, entering by the private, switchback road from the
corner of Crescent and Ramona, passing downhill to loop
below Kimberly Crest and into Prospect Park.

Leaving Prospect and going down Cajon, it was a replay of
the Rough Rider President's gallop, this time in an automobile
and going still faster.

Redlands boosters were not discouraged.

They would try for a Woodrow Wilson visit.

From the White House on April 2, 1915, the President replied
to John H. Fisher, president of the Redlands Chamber of
Commerce:

"I warmly appreciate the courtesy and cordial kindness of
your telegram of March thirtieth inviting me to visit Redlands
during my Western trip.

"I am sorry to say that it begins to look very doubtful whether
I shall be able to get away from Washington so long, at any

rate, as this war lasts with its daily problems for even neutral countries . . ."

Wilson's problems as the President of a neutral country would multiply until April 6, 1917. On that day the United States declared war on Germany.

The curtain had rung down forever on the era which had brought three Presidents to Redlands.

In the future, the railroads would not be used for mere good-will touring but for campaigning. The candidates would stick to the mainline routes, speaking from the rear platforms of their trains at the larger cities. For Redlanders that usually meant going to the Santa Fe station in San Bernardino.

Some appearances were notable for anecdote or, in contrast, for importance.

Campaigning to succeed Calvin Coolidge, Herbert Hoover paused in San Bernardino. It was evening. The crowd was large and friendly.

A local farmer elbowed his way through the throng until he could speak to Hoover. He had brought a little pig as a token of his esteem for the candidate and tried to hand it up to him. Lou Hoover, who never lacked for poise, intervened. She told the farmer that his gift was surely appreciated but the Hoovers had no way of keeping a pig on the train. Would he keep it for them until, perhaps, they could return to San Bernardino?

On the more serious side was the unique appearance of Harry Truman. He was President of the United States, having succeeded to the office upon the death of Franklin Roosevelt. The common wisdom in the spring of 1948 held that he didn't have a chance of being elected in November if he should be so foolish as to run.

Canny politician that he was, Truman decided to go to the people and make his own judgement. Arriving by train in San Bernardino one evening, he did not make a speech. Rather, he let the people in the crowd talk to him. He correctly sized up the mood of the nation from a series of crowd encounters and beat Governor Tom Dewey in the famous upset election of that year.

The railroad era had almost run out. Candidates would soon take to the air. If Redlanders would see Presidents at all, the occasions would have no resemblance to McKinley Day.

Such was the surprise appearance of Harry Truman on November 7, 1957. He and his wife, Bess, had been relaxing at Palm Desert. They had been the guests of Mon Wallgren, former governor of the state of Washington, and Mrs. Wallgren.

It was time for the Trumans to return to their home in Independence, Missouri. They would board the Santa Fe Super Chief at San Bernardino in the evening.

Although they had a late lunch at Palm Desert, the Trumans said they would like to have a snack before boarding the train. So their host telephoned Phil's Charcoal Broiler, a popular roadhouse on U.S. 99 (Redlands Boulevard) at the junction of Colton Avenue. He made reservations for five. The fifth member of the party was movie actor Phil Regan.

George Hesser, the proprietor, drew the curtains at one end of the dining room to give the party some privacy. But a former President cannot escape notice. Inevitably, a number of people spoke to him. That was easy since the Trumans were currently in the headlines as the nation's most popular "new" grandparents.

Polly Vasquez, Phil's hostess, told Truman that she was thrilled to see him at the Rams-Bears football game Sunday. She never dreamed that she would see him again in the same week and in Redlands at that.

It had been 6:30 when the group arrived, and the light supper did not take long.

About 200 gathered at the San Bernardino station. When the former President boarded the Super Chief he was given a basket of navel oranges.

While he was President, Dwight Eisenhower flew to California for golfing vacations, landing in Air Force One at Palm Springs. To see him, Redlanders had to go to the desert.

His wife, Mamie, did not like to fly: so in retirement he accommodated her by traveling by train. They arrived in San Bernardino from their Gettysburg home on December 21, 1961.

They disembarked from their special car on the Santa Fe, transferred to a limousine and headed for Palm Desert.

At that time the freeway had not been completed. They came through town on what would later be known as Redlands Boulevard. Folks who wanted to catch a glimpse of the Eisenhowers succeeded if they were standing at the Orange Street intersection at 8:13 A.M. That point is less than a block from the S.P. station where McKinley began his carriage tour.

Lyndon Johnson was probably in Redlands on one or more days in 1925. For a six-month period he lived only 10 miles away in San Bernardino. There he was the elevator operator in the Platt Building. He also clerked for an ex-Texan, attorney Thomas Martin.

Going down the homestretch of his 1964 campaign for the Presidency, Johnson returned rather triumphantly to San Bernardino on October 29.

Richard Nixon was in Redlands far more times than any other man who has been elected President. Part of this is explained by the fact that he is not only a Californian, but a native of nearby Orange County.

As a student at Whittier College, Nixon engaged in debates with University of Redlands opponents in 1932 and 1933. Also, as a second string player he sat on the bench during Whittier-Redlands football games.

In his successful campaign for United States Senator, "Dick," as he was then called, came to Redlands on May 6, 1950. The standard gambit for candidates in that campaign was to talk on street corners from station wagons.

At the Triangle, "Dick" was welcomed by Mayor Hugh Folkins who stands well over six feet. To set up a news picture for the *Facts* photographer, I levelled them as best I could, maneuvering Nixon up onto the curb and Folkins down into the gutter. No one objected, but I think there was a bit of laughter.

Nixon also spoke at the University of Redlands and went through the cafeteria line with students at the Commons. On October 19 he returned with his wife, Pat, for a breakfast rally at

La Posada Cafe on State just west of Orange.

Defeated by John Kennedy for the Presidency in 1960, he returned to California and ran unsuccessfully for governor. In that campaign he spoke at the University of Redlands on April 12, 1962. There he was greeted by Dr. Francis Thompson against whom he had debated in his Whittier College days.

Although he did not return to Redlands thereafter, he did make a dramatic appearance at Loma Linda on August 20, 1971. Arriving by helicopter, he walked to the speaker's platform to announce that a large veterans' hospital would be located there. The President was doing a favor for one of his strong Republican supporters in Congress, Jerry Pettis of Loma Linda.

Pettis was not destined to see the hospital. He died in an airplane accident. The hospital bears his name.

As a winter resident of Palm Desert, Gerald Ford may well have visited in Redlands, although I am unaware of any public appearance.

Plunging into politics in 1965, Ronald Reagan campaigned successfully for the office of Governor of California. Following standard practice for gubernatorial candidates, he visited newspaper editors up and down the state.

When he came to the *Redlands Daily Facts,* my brother, Bill, and I talked to him briefly. Then we turned him over to Ronald Kibby, reporter, who had asked for the interview. Ron asked him if his acting skills did not give him a special advantage in television appearances.

Reagan answered to the contrary. Television, he observed, presents the viewer with a close-up picture of a candidate. If the candidate is insincere — merely acting — the voter will see through the guise.

When Reagan walked out of the *Facts* office, something happened that I had never seen before with politicians. All the women in the front office almost swooned. Handsome Ron radiated 1,000 watts of sex appeal.

4

THE TIDES OF CHANGE

Houses, Houses, Houses

ON NOVEMBER 10, 1941, the *Redlands Daily Facts* published a double, banner headline across the top of page 1:

> Army Air Corps to Build $15-million
> Supply, Repair Depot Near Redlands.

To the community this was the most important news since Frank E. Brown and Edward G. Judson set out to establish the Redlands Colony.

As to the immediate outlook, the *Facts* correctly said: "This means that the defense and aviation boom — such as the one now raging in Riverside — will strike this region promptly."

As to the further outlook, the *Facts* foresaw "sudden growth in the permanent population of Redlands." This would be a drastic change. For 10 years the population had been static. The dead hand of the Great Depression was on the community and on its only major industry — citrus growing, shipping and selling.

Now Redlands would come to have a population in which many families would derive their income from a regular payroll. This would balance the local economy, ending the dependence on citrus alone.

As things turned out, the founding of what we now call Norton AFB was only the beginning of a permanent condition. The need for a powerful Air Force would not end with World War II, or Korea, or Vietnam. It would go on and on as long as Russian Communism continued to be a threat to the survival of America.

The Army Air Depot of World War II was destined to evolve and endure. This would transform the City of Redlands because of the facility's contribution to the population: active military, retired military, civilians employed by the military, and employees of all Air Force-support corporations.

In the past Redlanders had not seen whole housing tracts built at one time. Rather, land was usually subdivided and sold lot by lot to those who wished to have homes built, or to contractors who would build several houses on speculation.

The wave of the future was the housing tract. Developers would not only subdivide large parcels of land. They would build a house on every lot.

This revolution began within three months of the end of World War II. As early as November 1945 Attorney Russell Goodwin and Banker Ralph Seiersen, both of Redlands, launched the construction of 18 houses in a tract at the northwest corner of Colton and Church.

They were followed in May 1946 by Dunlap, Brummett and Demblon of South Pasadena who built their first 23 houses on Colton Avenue, eastward from the University campus. This was the first sign that many housing tracts would be built by out-of-town developers.

Demand for houses far exceeded the supply. The population had increased by 2,294 since 1940. The big post-war boom in housing tracts, however, would not get under way until construction materials were readily available.

Also responding to the continuing growth in population were the builders of large apartment complexes. Some of these projects were on a scale never seen here before.

In the boom year of 1963, construction started on 517 apartments and on 633 single-family dwellings. In 1986, approximately a thousand apartments were simultaneously under construction in the neighborhood of Barton Road and Alabama Street.

Shocked by the disappearance of orange groves and the appearance of vast apartment and housing tracts, the citizens began to clamor for growth control in 1976. That will be the subject of later comment.

Although the rate of growth is a controversial subject, there can be no doubt that city planning was vigorously pursued from the beginning of the new era.

Redlands engaged Charles W. Eliot, a planning consultant of national rank, to aid the beefed-up Planning Commission in developing a "general plan." The City would be carefully zoned to guide orderly development. The catch-phrase of the time was "a place for everything, and everything in its place."

With excellent foresight, Eliot said that new principal routes would be needed as the city grew. With planning, they could be created. Two conspicuous results are the westside artery, comprised of Tennessee and San Mateo streets, and the east-side thoroughfare, Ford/Judson.

Under the guidance of Eliot's successor, Simon Eisner, the Planning Commission continued to develop a concept of street patterns to accommodate the new housing tracts. The old-style grids were abandoned in favor of cul-de-sacs. Residential neighborhoods began to look quite different. The stubbed streets became, in effect, the front yards of the houses that faced them — favorite places for kids to play ball games. The cul-de-sacs also minimized the intersections of residential streets with main streets.

In the early period of the new Redlands, the City permitted developers to build streets in various locations that had neither curbs nor gutters. Either you like it or you don't. It's a matter of taste. However, in time, it became accepted practice to install curbs, gutters and sidewalks in tracts that are reasonably flat. The appearance of these subdivisions is neater.

But something happened when the tract builders sold the homes to private individuals. Board fences began to appear, separating the property of one family from the property of the next. Apparently there is a widespread passion for privacy, expressed in hundreds of walls and thousands of fences.

By the 1950s a new style of house began to dominate the tracts. It seemed to hug the ground since it was built on a concrete slab and had a low-pitched roof. It was never square but lineal — long in relation to its width. And the long side faced the street. The garage ceased to be a separate structure and was attached to the house.

California Ranch House (313 Marcia Street)

That came to be called "The California Ranch House" style although the roof was not red tile. Rather, the roof tended to be composition shingle or something new — grit, gravel and chunks of rock.

What the name meant was that the architect planned for outside as well as indoor living. At the back of the house a patio was provided for dining and barbecuing. Large glass doors opened the view of the patio and back garden.

Then a new madness developed — for private swimming pools. Before World War II, only a dozen homes had them. New materials, suitable pumps and filters, and easy financing changed that.

Swimming pool construction became an industry.

If you know Redlands only from a ground view, it is impossible to realize how many homes have pools in their rear yards. Take a low altitude flight over the town in a small plane and you will be amazed.

The interior of the so-called ranch house was more open than before. Even the kitchen would often open into the family room — a new kind of room — so mom could keep an eye on the kids if they were there.

The ranch house developed something that the bungalow had never had — "antlers." Television came in with a rush during the early 1950s. Every rooftop seemed to sprout an antenna. If aimed properly toward the transmitters on Mt. Wilson, they provided a new type of compass from which one could get direction — west. Eventually, cable television would serve many new houses, and the roof line would be clean.

By the 1970s it became obvious that the California Ranch House had serious shortcomings. It had neither a basement nor an attic. Where then, do you store all of those things that any household accumulates? You probably put all you can in the two-car garage. Yes, but if that fills the garage, where do you park the automobiles? You leave them on the driveway or on the street in front of your house.

The postwar era promptly brought a craze for recreational vehicles — 4-wheel drives, campers, travel trailers and motorcycles. Then came motorboats, sailboats, and all-terrain vehicles.

The neat, orderly subdivisions envisioned by the Planning Commission came to suggest used car lots. Thousands of vehicles are parked on the residential streets every night. Many of them are pickups that men use in their various occupations.

By the mid-1970s, quite a few houses were appearing with a double garage for cars and a third space to serve the purposes of an attic.

A second response was an innovation in business — the mini-storage facility. Row upon row of garage-like spaces could be rented to accommodate the overflow. Of course, the proliferation of apartment complexes also stimulated the demand for these facilities.

The spread of houses across the town created a need for new supermarkets to serve the people. Where should they be located? In old-style Redlands the larger food stores were found in the business district. Neighborhood markets were scattered in the residential areas.

It was the Planning Commission that decided supermarkets could well be built in locations out from the city center with a separation of at least one mile between them. They would have large parking lots. They became a dominant feature of the new Redlands. Most of the old, small, neighborhood stores could not compete and went out of business.

Controversy over mobile home parks did not boil up until about 1960. Should Redlands have them or should they all be built in the unincorporated areas? The Council asked for citizen opinion. Few people seemed interested. So the Council adopted a permissive ordinance. A developer soon appeared with a specific project. The roof almost blew off City Hall. So the Council threw the baby out with the bath and repealed the ordinance.

When things cooled down, a permissive ordinance was again adopted and several parks were developed. In the main, however, Yucaipa became the mobile home center of this region.

The Council's experience demonstrates that important policy cannot be formed until controversy forces citizens to pay attention and express their opinions. A city is not a society of philosophers.

King Orange Dethroned

W‍HEN THE FIRST orange groves were bought by subdividers, the citrus community was not unhappy.

"Old George got a nice price for his 10-acre piece, didn't he?" a grower might say. He, too, could look forward to a profitable sale of his own orchard if he chose to retire.

But disenchantment soon set in, especially among those who had never suffered through the anxious years of the Great Depression, worrying that they might lose their grove—and their livelihood—by foreclosure.

The orange groves added much to the charm of Redlands. After you drove out from town a bit, they were everywhere. In the residence districts many were bordered by box privet hedges. Often the owner and his family lived in a Queen Anne house in a corner of the grove.

The Planning Commission was concerned with preserving the orchards, not only as "greenbelts" but as the basis of the whole citrus industry. The fundamental problem, however, was that the City did not have the power to stop a grower from selling his private property or to require a new buyer to keep it in production. Furthermore, the City did not have the money or the will to save the orchards by buying them and farming them.

What realists could not say about the orchards was explained to me many years ago by Mark Anderson. He was manager of the Redlands-Highlands Fruit Exchange and familiar with hundreds of groves. He was also a shrewd observer of the Redlands scene.

"Frank," he began, "it's this way with Redlands orange groves.

"About one third are uneconomic. They never should have been planted.

"About one third are fair. They make money in good years and just get by the rest of the time.

"About one third are good groves farmed by good growers, and they make money just about every year."

The fate of the uneconomic groves was determined at the time they were planted – not at the time they were pulled out. You can see many of these relics in the Redlands Heights. As you drive up a mini-valley, you will notice on the slope above you what looks like the lines on a topographic map. That is land that was terraced for orange groves.

Some terraced orchards were excellent. Driving around the Redlands area you can still find some beautiful, productive trees. But many of the turn-of-the-century plantings were hard to irrigate, hard to fumigate for scale and hard to pick.

I was the dinner guest one evening of a Redlander who, I suspect, had lost a good deal of money developing terraced orchards. He was bitter. He insisted that the profit of orange growing is illusory. What prolonged the life of the industry, he rationalized, was a continuous infusion of new money by men who made their fortunes in the East, came West to escape the disagreeable winters and bought orange groves before they knew anything about them.

There is some truth in his story, exaggerated though it was.

But many formerly economic orange groves did begin to decline after 1950. The annual production went down.

The popular explanation for this trend was easy to learn. Talk to almost any grower and you could bet five-to-one that he would blame smog. This recently identified villain was at the top of every man's list.

A major cause of the decline was certainly "The Speculative Effect." Let me explain.

As the demand for subdividable land continued, many growers became certain that in a few years they would be selling out. While holding on for a higher price, they did not try to keep their orchards in tip-top condition.

Five years later, however, they might find that the market for groves had collapsed. They were stuck with run-down orchards.

One veteran citrus man told me that the moral to this sad tale was: "Keep right on farming, the best you know how, until the day you sell and your deal comes out of escrow."

"The Speculative Effect" was intensified by the provisions of the Internal Revenue Code. An orange grove became a popular tax shelter. It seemed that investors with plenty of money to risk could buy orange groves and hang on to them for some time. The crop returns would pay the cost of farming. When land prices had risen appreciably, thanks to the steady development of the Redlands area, the investor would sell out at a neat profit.

Many of these sales collapsed because the groves did not pay their own way. If they were "Mickey Mouse Deals," with little or no money up front, the easiest way out for the investor was to turn the property back to the original owner.

"The Speculative Effect" had two other important influences on the citrus industry.

One was the invasion of citrus by large corporations whose main business is far removed from agriculture. Mobil Oil's land development subsidiary bought the vast acreage of the East Highlands Orange Company. Pacific Lighting — parent of Southern California Gas Company — purchased a substantial bloc of orchards at Greenspot, northeast of Mentone.

At the same time, much acreage passed from the ownership of local men who managed their own groves to absentee owners whose interest was tax sheltering.

This resulted in the formation of one very large farming company and increased business for established grove contractors.

The old order had changed. No longer did the butcher, the baker and the candlestick maker own groves, farm them, and endlessly talk about them.

At the same time, citriculture was undergoing much change. In the past, the only way to irrigate a grove was by running water down furrows. A better way, it was found, was to distribute water through hoses and apply it with small sprinklers or emitters. Less water was required. The crops, in many groves were better. And one man could irrigate far more acreage.

Instead of laboriously distributing manure from a truck, chemical fertilizer could be applied with the irrigation water.

Pruning was no longer a hand job. Huge machines with whirling saws on booms crawled down the rows and hedged, or topped, the trees with remarkable speed.

If the conversion of groves to subdivisions—or just to open land—was spectacular, the rapid disappearance of packing houses was even more so.

There were obvious reasons.

As anyone could see by driving around Redlands, the acreage that had been producing oranges had shrunk dramatically.

Not visible in like manner, however, was the shrinking yield from the groves that remained in production. There were several influences, such as "The Speculative Effect" and the aging of groves that for many years had been poorly farmed. Some crops were notable for the small sizes of the fruits—sizes that the market does not want.

Historically, the Redlands district needed a lot of packing houses because the fruit was hauled from the groves by horse and wagon. What was the efficient radius one house could serve? Three miles . . . four miles? So there were houses in Crafton, downtown Redlands and Bryn Mawr.

Although the distance factor became much less important when trucks replaced wagons, the hauling was still done in field boxes of a size that one man could hoist onto a truck. Also, there

were ranch trucks that could drive down the
rows and load from each set.

The old method could not endure in the
face of rising costs. Large wooden bins
replaced the relatively small field boxes.
They could be picked up with a fork lift,
moved to an over-the-road "semi" and
zipped off to a packing house in Riverside or
Corona.

Orange Field Box

While economic forces were bound to eliminate many old
packing houses, the decline was hastened by fires. One plant
after another went up in smoke.

From the earliest days, packing houses had always been sited
on railway lines. The great markets for oranges were scattered
across the whole continent. The only way to ship the fruit was in
refrigerated box cars.

By the 1930s, however, railroads began to lose packing house
business to trucks. Boxes of fruit could be loaded here and delivered directly to customers — in California and Arizona first, and
then to more distant places. It was easier to sell oranges in
smaller lots than in the 462-box lots of the railroad refrigerator
car.

What had been a trickle of diversion to trucks before World
War II became a river. Finally, there was no business for the
Southern Pacific, and the branch line into Redlands from the
main line at Bryn Mawr was abandoned. The Pacific Electric,
serving two houses on San Bernardino Avenue, gave up.

At this writing, the Santa Fe line still maintains its track from
San Bernardino to Redlands and Mentone to deliver lumber,
mid-Western grain for the poultry feed mills, and other freight.

Today a large volume of Redlands shipments go only a short
distance by truck — to the docks at Los Angeles Harbor. From
there the cartons are carried by ship to Hong Kong. The Chi-
nese love the fruit our navel trees produce — smooth, thin-
skinned, fairly round, small and sweet. They are willing to pay a
premium for them.

Downtown Comes Unglued

On July 25, 1899, Redlander Cass Gaylord drove his horseless carriage, "Tommy," about town, causing much excitement. Clerks and patrons poured out of stores. A flock of boys on bicycles followed the primitive automobile — the first in the city.

Gaylord's sensational ride was the precursor of the first-stage transformation of Downtown. Most of the visible change occurred on the streets where the carriages were replaced by automobiles. The buildings did not change much in appearance, although livery stables tended to become garages.

For nearly 50 years Redlands was largely able to ignore the implications of the automobile for the future of the business district. There came to be some shortage of parking on the streets but it was not, at first, acute. Downtown could be taken for granted. It was.

Two chapters in Redlands history delayed the awakening for one full generation.

First — the Great Depression. For a decade the city was paralyzed by it. Parking facilities that were adequate in 1930 were adequate in 1940.

Second — The status quo continued to be satisfactory until the end of the 1940s. During the war, gasoline was rationed, so people did as little driving as they could. Also, no cars were manufactured during the war. Afterwards it took Detroit a couple of years to gear up to full capacity.

But by 1949 the growth of the population was beginning to pinch Downtown. There was but little off-street parking. Wasn't a lot more needed?

A detailed study gave this answer: "No, not if all the available on-street parking is efficiently used."

Alas, there is a quirk in human nature that makes efficient use of parking an idle dream. Early attempts at strict enforcement of the regulations often resulted in the ticketing of the very merchants whose business success hinged on patrons being able to stop in front of their stores.

Parking meters were installed as the next remedy. No one really liked them even though they did improve the rate of turnover at the curbs. There is something about parking that reaches deep into the human personality. In extreme cases, the parking meter seemed to be taken as an insult to a citizen's social status.

The ultimate irate motorist was an out-of-town labor lawyer who happened to park on State Street and overstay the time for which he had deposited coins. He fought his parking ticket all the way to the United States Supreme Court. The Justices failed to find any great Constitutional issue in his appeal and denied him a hearing.

What did lead to the creation of off-street parking lots, one after another, was the establishment of a Downtown Parking District with policies set by an able Board of Commissioners. Although they moved as rapidly as financial resources permitted, there always seemed to be too little space too late.

The Planning Commission was not asleep at the switch. An ordinance was adopted by the City requiring that plans for new buildings include adequate parking spaces for employees and patrons.

From personal experience I can tell you how that forced some expanding businesses to relocate outside the Core Area.

My brother, Bill, and I owned the *Redlands Daily Facts*. The newspaper had been published for a half-century in a long but narrow building at Citrus and Fifth in the very heart of Downtown. By the early 1950s we needed a rotary press to accommodate our growing circulation. That, in turn, led to the need for an entirely new building.

Since the business district was already built up, there was no open parcel we could build on. Nor was it within our resources to assemble parcels and demolish the structures that happened to be on them.

The nearest feasible site was at Center and Brookside, a half-mile from the Central Business District. Because it was part of an orange grove, we could afford to buy it. The generous amount of land was adequate for the building, for parking and for landscaping. Our lawns and trees became the standard for the office buildings that were later built to the west of us on Brookside.

Like the Moore brothers, many entrepreneurs would have preferred a Downtown location but the economics of land drove them outside. The result by now — 1987 — has been a remarkable scatteration of businesses and services west of Texas Street.

The City Council did try to provide space for new commercial buildings on State Street, just west of the present Mall. A Redevelopment Agency was created and it developed a detailed plan for removing the houses, resubdividing the land and offering the parcels as construction sites for private businesses.

Unfortunately, the proposal was premature. Redevelopment was a new scheme in California. No project had been completed for Redlanders to see and to study. Furthermore, the City had no money to spare because so many capital improvements were needed to catch up on long-delayed maintenance and to provide facilities for the enlarged population. The Council rejected the plan in 1952. There were higher priorities.

At this time an entirely new scheme for retail shopping began to appear elsewhere in California. It was called "a shopping center." The term was so new than that it had to be explained to anyone who had never seen one. Today, everyone knows what the term means.

The shopping center concept frightened the daylights out of the business and political community of Redlands. The threat to Downtown was clear and real.

Responding to the threat, the community established an ad hoc committee to diagnose the problem and to prescribe the remedy. Once started, this process was to continue until the day when skeptics were saying "Downtown has been studied to death."

A high peak was reached in 1964 when the prestigious Los Angeles firm of planning consultants — Victor Gruen and Associates — presented a brilliant report. A possible Central City Development Project was proposed, with a detailed analysis to support it.

"Competition from decentralized regional shopping centers is usually identified as the cause of downtown's troubles," Gruen wrote. "This, in turn, is the outgrowth of deep-rooted central area problems in the form of obsolete buildings, traffic congestion, inadequate parking, and unattractive environment.

"Today, Downtown Redlands has the appearance of a stable and healthy business district. However, the San Bernardino-Riverside area will in the very near future develop new business and shopping magnets within reasonable driving time of Redlands. Failure of Downtown to meet the future needs of existing and potential commercial enterprises will cause the threat of economic blight to become a reality."

Gruen made a critical mistake. The consultants believed that the Central City could be revitalized without resort to an Urban Renewal Program. As we shall presently see, this proved to be untrue.

Furthermore, the Gruen study was strong on diagnosis but flawed on prescription. The plan called for abandoning State as an automobile street and converting it into a pedestrian mall. The medicine was disastrous where taken, as in Riverside. Redlands' inability to implement that phase of Gruen was a blessing in disguise.

Gruen's optimism with regard to privately undertaken redevelopment may have been encouraged by what turned out to be a misleading sign. Financier C. Arnholt Smith of San Diego was aggressively expanding the U.S. National Bank. He wanted to open a branch in Redlands. Taking a cue from Gruen he decided to develop an entire block while he was about it.

The excavation in 1964 for underground parking was enormous — all of the block which City Hall faces. Over this, the Redlands Plaza was built with the bank at the corner. The facade was in the trademark style of U.S. National—country rock facing, and tall, square, marble pillars.

Smith's dream fizzled. The Plaza did not attract the tenants needed to make the project pay out. In 1977 the bank sold the development to private individuals who later sold it to the City. The U.S. National chain became troubled, merged with Crocker and Crocker, in turn, merged with Wells Fargo.

In 1968, "Town Square" emerged. West State Street would be redeveloped with the Harris department store as anchor. Super-enthusiasts even staged a groundbreaking. A strange silence followed; no construction began. Although I was editor of the *Facts* at the time, I did not learn for 17 years what had truly happened. The Harris company did not sign the lease that would make Town Square fly. The project collapsed.

Finally, one man was responsible for bringing the years of frustration over Downtown to an end. He is Jack B. Cummings, a 1950 graduate of the University of Redlands and later the director of Alumni Relations. Wishing to advance in the academic world, he decided to study for a master's degree. His mentor, Prof. Robert Morlan, a former member of the City Council, steered him onto the topic of Urban Redevelopment agencies.

Elected to the City Council in 1964, Cummings shared the public frustration over the Gruen fiasco and the failure of Town Square. But armed with the information he had acquired in qualifying for his M.A. degree in 1965, he correctly saw that the City had to again go the Redevelopment Agency route. Teamed with a strong City Manager, Pete Merritt, Jr., he pulled it off.

From Orange to Eureka, obsolete buildings were torn down. These included such landmarks as the massive La Posada Hotel and the Greek Revival bank building at Orange and State. The Elks gave up their large clubhouse and relocated on New York Street.

Although the opportunity for federal financing had expired, the Redevelopment Agency managed the considerable feat of selling bonds on the open market. Ground was broken in December, 1975, and the Redlands Mall opened in March

1977, with the Harris' department store as anchor.

The next most visible project was the construction in 1980–81 of the six-story, corporate headquarters of Redlands Federal Savings and Loan on east State. This fulfilled the dream of President J. Edward Harp who had played a leading role in developing a local business into a regional institution with 14 branches. Of first-class design and construction, the building set a new standard for Redlands.

You might be interested to know that I am writing this book in my fifth-floor office of "Red Fed." My view extends from town to the heights. Surprisingly, most of the houses are hidden in a veritable forest of ornamental trees.

Under the determined leadership of the first woman mayor of Redlands, Carole Beswick, the Redevelopment Agency undertook its second major project in 1985. East State Street was beautified by repaving the sidewalks with red bricks and creating a new/old-fashioned look with vintage street lights and sidewalk benches.

Unperturbed by the heated criticisms of how the State Street project was carried out, the Council went on in 1986 to push the

State Street

revitalization of Orange Street, just south of the freeway. At the time of this writing the highly controversial project is beginning to unfold.

During the late 1950s the City engaged in an exercise inspired by the fable, "The Emperor Wears No Clothes." The pretense was that no shopping center had been allowed to develop. But the fact was that Milton Sage built an enormous supermarket, well out from Downtown, on Redlands Boulevard at Cypress. No store on such a scale had previously existed here.

Sage said proudly during construction: "In this store you will be able to buy everything you need, although not everything that you may want."

The store opened on November 2, 1959, and was an instant commercial success. "Sage's" became a Redlands byword. In six stages of development, a mall, "Citrus Village," was added and spaces were leased to a variety of tenants ranging from a barber shop to a bank.

In an overly ambitious venture, Sage opened a large store, "Milton's," featuring high fashion wear for women. He did not have the necessary merchandising experience in that field.

Sage's luck ran out. He had gone out on a financial limb to develop an empire in Riverside, San Bernardino and Redlands. It collapsed. Felled by a heart attack, he was in no physical condition to make a comeback.

In 1973 his great Sage's market became "Lucky's." The store that had been "Milton's" was leased to Webb's of Glendale and a junior department store was operated there for about 13 years. Citrus Village went into decline but in 1986 was thoroughly overhauled.

In spite of any policy that "City Hall" might adopt to protect Downtown, lands to the west would inevitably attract major retailing development. Because much of the property was in citrus, large parcels could be assembled. They are in proximity to Interstate 10 at Alabama and at Tennessee.

Salivating over the juicy sales taxes that would accrue to the municipality, the Council sanctioned the huge K-Mart Store.

Tri-City Center, with several large retailers and many small ones, followed. Automobile dealers also gravitated west.

Cass Gaylord started the whole process in 1899 when he drove his Haynes-Apperson about the streets of Redlands. Business could not be contained forever in Downtown, a creation of the horse-and-buggy days.

Farewell, Old School

"THE KINGSBURY ELEMENTARY SCHOOL was almost in our back yard," Dr. Larry Burgess explained. "In 1969 I was not living here because I was studying for my degree at Claremont Graduate School.

"When I came home I was horrified. They were demolishing my school with a wrecking ball. They were taking away my memories. I wept."

Dr. Burgess was not alone. In the period from 1956 to 1970, thousands of Redlanders saw the schoolhouses of their memories torn down.

Today, in 1987, only a few buildings that were standing before World War II can still be seen. Redlands schools — private as well as public — have been rebuilt, or built anew.

This is surprising in view of the reluctance of citizens to vote for any proposition that will increase their taxes. It tells you that education of our children is their first priority outside of the home.

Yes, but how is it possible to convince people who may live in an older home to go along with the replacement of a schoolhouse that seems to have decades of remaining life? There is no secret here. It is a simple fact that parents and school authorities are supersensitive to the structural safety of the buildings in which children attend school. They do not let sentiment stand in the way of a wrecking crew.

They also respond vigorously to overcrowding, especially if it results in double sessions, or — horror of horrors — triple sessions, as was the case for a time at the high school.

Since the school system sorely needed more and more classrooms in the post-War era, why did the trustees order any buildings torn down? That question has a two-part answer.

Starting in 1949 the trustees launched a building program at the high school. All seemed to be going well for about four years. Then a state inspector took a careful look at the main building, from basement to attic. "There is little to commend it from an earthquake-safety standpoint," he said in his report.

In the summer of 1956 the 53-year-old structure was torn down. Many men and women who had happy memories of their high school days took it hard. They consoled themselves by having an artist fashion a suitable china plate. Overall, it is white, with a gold rim. The majestic Administration Building, with its commanding site and ivy-covered walls, is sketched in blue.

The second round of demolitions was triggered in the most roundabout way. During the early 1960s the California Legislature recodified the law of torts. When the School Board's attorney read it under a microscope, so to speak, he reached a startling conclusion. Each member of the School Board would be personally liable for the injury or death of a child in an earthquake-collapsed building unless the trustees had made every effort to avoid a catastrophe.

A structural engineer, who was promptly hired, concentrated on the buildings which dated to about 1926. To the layman they looked as strong as forts. They were built with reinforced concrete walls and red tile roofs. Unfortunately for the taxpayers, they were designed before the lessons of the Long Beach (1933) earthquake had been learned and codified in the Field Act.

Their chief fault was this. The roof structures simply rested on the walls. Gravity held them in place.

In an earthquake, however, walls move back and forth. If they shift out from under the roof, it will cave in. In a Field Act building the walls and roof must be structurally tied together. Except for the Clock Auditorium at the high school, this could not be accomplished retroactively.

A great many Redlands citizens were incredulous of the engineering report. To this day, many are unwilling to believe it was necessary to raze Redlands Junior High, Kingsbury, Franklin and Crafton. I understand their sentimental attachment to those handsome, "Spanish-style" buildings, but I climbed ladders with the engineer, looked, and verified to my own satisfaction the truth of what he was saying.

The replacement of this set of buildings was financed by a bond issue which included many other school construction projects.

It is ironic that Clock could be salvaged and much improved. A noted Los Angeles architect, Edwin Bergstrom, originally designed a magnificent auditorium for the high school, but the plan was too costly and was rejected. He then stripped away all the amenities and all the architectural features which would have given it classical style. The revised plan was adopted, and the Ugly Duckling auditorium was built.

The notion that school buildings should be architecturally impressive ended in that era — the prosperous 1920s. The public mood shifted during the Great Depression. The hard-pressed taxpayers were ready for a revolutionary style in which the function of the building would govern the design. Marsh, Smith and Powell of Los Angeles gave them the prototype in the McKinley School, 1938.

No more two-story buildings with inside halls and corridors. The new style was low — one story. The corridors were outdoors — nothing but a cement floor and a roof overhead. The classrooms were entered directly. One wall, being almost entirely comprised of windows, admitted much light.

In the post-War era, a new school would often be broken up into a number of classroom units, plus a hall and an office. A typical building is of frame and stucco, with a low-pitched roof. Schools became so nondescript that I wonder if anyone will ever shed tears when one is eventually torn down.

Decoration is rare. Architect Paul Ulmer did manage to place simple mosaics — seals, llamas, dolphins and giraffes — on Kimberly buildings. But Cope Junior High is another story.

Three artists worked for months to create mosaics to be placed on the outside of Campbell Hall. One conventional set presented such themes as agriculture in local history. But the other

— and much larger — display was too "modernistic" for the Philistines of Redlands. Space ships, lightning bolts and wild blue yonder created so much criticism that the picture was removed.

The one-story buildings proved, by the test of time, to have a major fault. The architects assumed too much goodness in mankind. They did not realize that schools are magnets for vandals — that break-ins must be expected. Nor were they cynical enough to anticipate that some vandals would be arsonists.

The School Board received an appropriate architectural response in the design of the Franklin School (1971). This is a veritable fort — a double doughnut. Walk entirely around the outside and you will find no windows; they face inward. The entrance which admits you to the holes in the doughnuts is closed, during non-school hours, with a mighty gate. The earth-tone block walls suggest adobe.

The Franklin School is located about a half-mile due west of the University of Redlands. In the early post-War period, the School Board secretly bought land on Occidental Street, less than a mile away, for a new elementary school. The trustees thought the price on any land they sought to purchase would be raised if they made their intentions public.

But the public simply would not stand for the Occidental site.

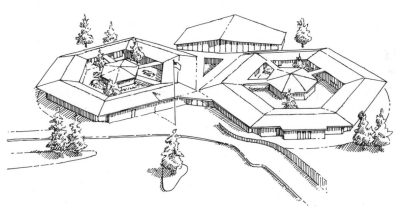

Franklin School

It was too close to Franklin and too far from the homes in the Lugonia district to be served. In the end, the trustees had to unscramble the omelet by selling the land. What started out as a strategy of economy backfired into a costly mistake.

As a former newspaperman, I dwell on this case history because my experience taught me that sound public decisions have to be made in public. Officials need feedback from the citizenry to check their own judgements and to appreciate the views of their constituents.

Two cardinal and related policies evolved in the School Board. First, the Redlands Junior High School plant would be demolished for earthquake-safety reasons. Instead of one junior high, there would be three. Secondly, a "north campus" at the high school would be developed on the former junior high site.

The decentralization of the junior high occurred in an era in which the public increasingly expected that after-school recreation would be provided on public grounds.

Eventually, playgrounds would be turfed and they would be used for organized sports — especially baseball and soccer — after school hours and on Saturdays. By public demand, turfing of playgrounds extended to the elementary schools.

When it came to naming the new schools, there was no interest in the heroes of American history. Indeed, the "Lincoln" name was allowed to lapse without a whimper. Rather, the preference was for local citizens. All of the junior highs were so named.

Edward M. Cope served on the School Board for 29 years and was a stalwart of the American Red Cross. As a superintendent of schools, Henry G. Clement was a strong leader. Editor Paul W. Moore of the *Redlands Daily Facts* and his successor sons, Bill and Frank, were all-weather supporters of the public school system.

When the building industry revived after World War II, Mentone was the local hot spot. The new school which opened there in 1949 was automatically given the place-name, "Mentone."

"Mariposa" is also a place-name — but not quite so logical.

The story here is that the School Board expected, at first, to build the new plant at the eastern end of Mariposa Drive. The name became attached to the plan and stuck with it when a site on Palo Alto Drive was chosen instead.

In attempting to name the new elementary school on Cypress Avenue, the School Board fumbled. The trustees tried to call it "Terracina." But the location is neither on Terracina Boulevard nor is it in the historic Terracina district.

George Ide, the greatest worshipper of local heroes in all of Redlands history, figuratively mounted his horse and charged. He would have none other than "Smiley." Not only were the Smiley brothers the patron saints of Redlands, the school site is situated about a mile from Smiley Heights, the private park that brought early fame to Redlands. The trustees knew when they were licked. They surrendered.

The new elementary school on South Avenue was named for Helen Cheney Kimberly (Mrs. John A.). She was determined that young women should develop their potential for community leadership. In 1916 — four years after women became voters in California — she founded the Kimberly Juniors as an adjunct of the Contemporary Club to give such training.

Since there was no new high school, naming became internal at the existing school. The new auditorium of intermediate size was named in honor of Grace Mullen, the redoubtable founder of the Redlands Community Music Association. The new shop building took the name of Clarence G. Hardy. Highly respected, he taught manual arts at the high school for 39 years.

Now I must confess to having had a hand in selecting another name.

I abhor the term "multipurpose room," beloved by professional educators. It is gobbledygook. Fearing that it would again be used at the high school, I studied dictionaries and concluded that the prospective building would simply be a "hall." The term "Terrier" had been given a strong and popular connotation by the frequent victories of the football team. Putting the two words together, I knew I had a winner.

The Student Council jumped for it like a trout for a fly. The School Board said, "OK."

With the popularity of "Terrier" as a building name established, it carried forward to the new gymnasium. That building deserves further mention.

A wave of fear swept over the nation when the Russians began to build the Berlin Wall in 1961. In Redlands, many people put underground bomb shelters in their own back yards. Various public buildings were identified as safe shelters and were so marked.

The School Board realized that the proposed gymnasium might also serve as a bomb shelter if built underground. The architect who had the job made a study of the scheme and reported to the trustees. They decided, after all, on a conventional design.

For years the high school swimming team had used the YMCA pool for training. One member of the School Board insisted that students should have a facility of their own. He is Brig. Gen. Richard L. Scott. Both he and his wife were devoted to marathon workouts in their own pool. Scott prevailed; two pools were built.

Within the public system, three specialized schools were established.

One of them was a response to a dilemma in California education. Boys and girls are required to attend school until they are 18. Yet, some of them are round pegs in square holes at Redlands High School. For their special needs, an alternative high school was developed so they could profitably continue their educations.

The students chose the name themselves. They were getting out a little paper which they called "The Orange Crate." When they needed a name for their school—well, why not "Orangewood"? In a citrus town it is apt.

"Orangewood" found a permanent home in the former Lincoln Elementary School on Texas Street.

The other special schools are located in Redlands but serve

students from other districts as well.

Heisner School for the Handicapped operates in its own plant on the Mission Elementary School grounds, Redlands Boulevard at California Street. The name honors former Superintendent of Schools Fred Heisner whose great interest was stimulated by his own wheelchaired son.

A therapy pool was built at the Crafton School — the first location of the handicapped — by the Kiwanis Club of Redlands. In 1972 operations shifted to Heisner where, again, an exercise pool was built.

Training men and women for entry level jobs in the world of everyday work is the Regional Occupation School. It has an unusual home in the former Stevens Hosiery mill on Tennessee Street.

The era of expansion in the public school system has been accompanied by a parallel growth in private schools. Nine are operating presently — that is, in 1987.

Seven are church related. The "grandfather" of them all is the Sacred Heart School on Eureka Street, situated just south of the Catholic Church of the same name.

The Redlands Christian School has a large plant adjacent to the First Christian Reformed Church on North Church Street. It is a reminder to the general community of the many people of Dutch ancestry who live here.

The vigor of the Seventh-Day Adventist Church is indicated by the size of the Redlands Junior Academy on Tennessee Street.

New private schools usually start in makeshift quarters. Calvary Chapel of Redlands is currently occupying the basement of the former Crown Jewel packing house, Alabama Street at San Bernardino Avenue.

In 1957 Valley Preparatory School opened in a brick house on Mountain View Road, south of Redlands Boulevard. Anson Van Leuven built it at the end of the Mill Creek Zanja in 1857 or 1858. Now within the city limits of Loma Linda, it is one of the oldest buildings in the county.

Valley Prep found its permanent home in 1959 on Ford Street, south of South Avenue. There it has grown into the largest private, secular school in town.

The movement to start a Montessori school jelled with such unexpected speed in 1976 that the founders had to provide a home as quickly as they could. At Irvine, in Orange County, they found a 36-by 60-foot structure in a shopping center that had been used by a bank. They moved it, intact, to New York Street in Redlands. Within five weeks of arrival, it was made ready for pupils.

The enrollment has grown to 230. There are three moved-in structures and one which was built on the site. "Where do we go from New York Street?" the leaders are asking themselves.

Topping all other stories of this kind, is the astounding one of the Fallsvale Elementary School . . . of the fierce pride that the community takes in it . . . and of the prodigious feat of the people in building classrooms for their children when the school district failed them.

Situated in the forested bottom of deep Mill Creek Canyon, Forest Falls attracts many people in summer but has a small, all-year population. Most of the residents commute to jobs in the valley. They are willing to do this because they love the forest, the grandeur of the mountains, and their tight-knit community.

Although Forest Falls is within the Redlands Unified School District, it is remote. The distance from the school superintendent's office is 17 miles.

Stone Fallsvale School

Trouble began when the stone schoolhouse built in 1932 was condemned. The engineering judgment was that it would fail in an earthquake. This was not to be taken lightly in a canyon that owes its origin to an earthquake fault and erosion.

The school district could not finance construction by the standard method—a contract awarded to a low bidder. In this situation the Forest Falls people were adamant against having their children bussed down to the valley. It took a special act of the Legislature to keep the stone building in use during the two years required to work out the problem.

Confronted with a seemingly insoluble problem, the people made an extraordinary decision. If the district would provide the materials, they would provide the labor.

This compromise was formalized in a contract with Robert Tobias, a Forest Falls resident. But he could find only one company willing to post a performance bond—a guarantee to the district that the volunteers would complete the project. Furthermore, the company insisted on collateral.

Faced with a four-day deadline, Forest Falls leaders such as Tom McIntosh worked day and night. Seventeen families mortgaged their homes in the amount of $10,000 apiece. The deal was complete.

The architect had designed two classroom buildings with materials volunteers could handle. The walls are of laminated planks, six inches thick and varnished rather than painted outside. The wooden construction is conspicuous.

Luck favors the bold. A man in San Gabriel who was in charge of a California Conservation Corps crew chanced to see

New Fallsvale School

on television the Forest Falls volunteers at work. The CCCs adopted the project. With their help, a job that would have taken two years was completed in eight months. In January, 1982, the pupils moved in. There are currently 56 children in three classrooms in six grades.

Emotion shook Robert Tobias when he spoke before the School Board on October 12, 1982. He said:

"God's hand was in this project. Many prayers were answered from beginning to end."

Churches in All Directions

NOT TO BE OUTDONE by the subdividers, the school system, and business entrepreneurs, the Christians of Redlands went on a building spree as soon as they could after World War II.

The boom lasted for more than twenty years.

Never again would Redlands look the same.

Down came many of the picturesque old buildings with their belfries and steeples. The wreckers got some. The movers hauled others away. Fires finished the rest.

While a few congregations stuck to their long-established locations in Central Redlands, the rest went in all directions. They found sites to the north, east, south and west. The Planning Commission did not blow the whistle on them because there was no Church Zone in the City Plan.

While scattering in all directions, the Christians did not look to Europe — the model in earlier times — for architectural inspiration. They did not try to imitate the cathedrals as their fathers had. They skipped the mandatory gothic windows of yesteryear. They may even have laughed at the false buttresses which were applied in 1882 to the first church ever built in present-day Redlands — the Terrace Congregational Church on Terrace at Church Street.

With no interest in traditional styles, they asked their architects to design churches which would have the most utility for the fewest dollars.

Before going on to consider why these things happened, let's pause to look at important landmarks — two old, one new.

While the Congregationalists built and own the red brick building at the Lord's Corner — Cajon and Olive — it belongs to everybody. Here is the square tower which holds aloft the four-sided "town clock." Here is the great bell which in clanging out

Congregational Church Tower   *First Baptist Church Tower*

the hour has been heard as far away as Bryn Mawr. And here, also, are those seductive chimes that can make you stop your car for a moment to listen, to enjoy and perhaps to sing.

The style of the building speaks clearly of the turn-of-the-century when it was built. You can close your eyes and imagine ladies stepping out of carriages in dresses that swept the sidewalk. You can almost hear the motorman of the Smiley Heights streetcar ringing his bell.

I would like to say that this church is of an original design — stone at the foot of the brick walls, large gothic windows (one by Tiffany Studios), and stone-decorated archways at the entrance. But it is almost a copy of a Congregational church in San Diego by the same architects, Hebbard and Gill.

Why has this Victorian gem survived? Because the Congregationalists were able to buy land for a parking lot, for the construction of Kimberly Hall and for their Sunday School. Oh, yes — and they had a bit of luck, too. They escaped the fire that destroyed two nearby churches.

Also right out of a turn-of-the-century picture book is Trinity Episcopal Church. It was located on Fern Avenue, a block west of the noisy streetcars on Cajon Street, in 1903.

Squint your eyes a little and ask yourself: "Where am I? Could I really be in an English country village?" The architecture says, "Yes, you could be."

Facing the church, you see walls which are unique in Redlands. They are of cut, Santa Ana Wash granite, and buttressed. Mrs. Albert C. Burrage, who gave the $20,000 necessary to build Trinity, was partial to stone and required it. But the walls are pictorially overwhelmed by the massive, steep, shingled roof.

For another English touch you'll find half-timbering under the gables.

You won't, however, see the massive, square tower that architect Daniel F. Willard provided, "in the English tradition," on his blueprints.

It should have been there, of course, because the Episcopalians had a steeple on their first church which was built on Center below Cypress, and then moved to the Lord's Corner (YWCA site) for use from 1896 to 1904. Surprise, surprise! The contractor's first bid was too high. To get the cost down to $19,680, the Fern Avenue tower was sacrificed.

For three years the new church was without gas for heating and electricity for lighting. Did some parishioners wear long drawers in January? And could the poor illumination have been the source of an amused expression — "Dim religious light" — which one member, my father, used throughout his life?

Although other congregations turned their backs on historic styles after World War II, members of the First Baptist Church did not.

Their first decision, though, was not architecture but site. Instead of fleeing from the Central City, they chose to tear down their Victorian sanctuary at the Lord's Corner and rebuild on the same ground in 1952. They were strongly committed to this place by the decision they made in 1926 to augment their facilities with auxiliary buildings extending westward to Fourth Street.

Now allow me a poetic observation about how one architect, who loved the Spanish style, passed the torch to another. One was just before the War; the other was just afterwards.

The first architect designed St. Mary's Catholic Church and appropriately gave it Spanish features for Spanish-speaking people. As the wording on the cornerstone puts it: "This church was built by the Mexican people of Redlands for the Glory of God . . . Dedicated October 1941." (The building was moved to a new site on Columbia Street, and enlarged, in 1986.)

The second architect, Frederick Kennedy, Jr. of Pasadena, may have been completely unaware of St. Mary's, but he surely knew about Bertram Goodhue. He was an unabashed admirer and called him "the greatest architect the United States ever produced." As did many other Southern California architects, Kennedy fell under the lasting spell of Goodhue's buildings for the Panama-Pacific Exposition of 1916 in Balboa Park, San Diego.

The most prominent features of St. Mary's and First Baptist are their towers, topped with colorful tile domes. Kennedy built his as tall as he claimed the Uniform Building Code allowed, which was 71 feet. He also elaborated it with balconies, iron railings and pyramid-shaped ornaments.

Two years later the Spanish influence made a final appearance in the First Christian Reformed building on Church Street. The style is more California Mission than San Diego Exposition. Since most of the parishioners are of Dutch ancestry, you might expect their church to speak more of Holland than of Mission San Luis Rey, but members of the present generation are as thoroughly "California-ized" as other Redlanders.

Although Father Junipero Serra, founder of the California Missions, was a great walker, the post-War Redlanders were not. They had become an automobile people, through and through. This had a strong impact on the churches.

Before the War, church-goers could park their cars at the curbs. Indeed, they had to because church lots were rare. But the City, at long last, decreed that any new church had to be accompanied by off-street parking. In the Central City this was not financially possible. The real estate was too expensive.

So the churches did what business did — scatter. Usually the site chosen was in an orange grove because the price was right and there was but one owner with whom to bargain.

Yes, but could a church be located at almost any place outside of the Central City? Would members be willing to drive across town to worship? It took five years to demonstrate that the answer was "yes." Only one preacher of my acquaintance — the one whose church was farthest out from town — confessed to me that his location was inconvenient.

When the Christians fled from the Central City they left behind them their notions of how a proper church should look. At the Lord's Corner, for example, all three of the venerable churches had belfries. Many members lived near enough to hear the bells.

But in their outlying locations the churches could not reach the ears of their members. Belfries were functionally obsolete. They disappeared. In their place some churches erected pylons to hold the cross on high.

Nor did the new-style churches have to have massive side walls in which to display large, stained glass windows with Biblical figures. On the contrary, a few have such low walls you have to look to see if they actually exist.

The most popular style of the post-War era is dominated by its roof. Viewed head-on, it is as simple in outline as the capital letter "A". The two slopes rise to a long ridge, so sharp that you could put a saddle on it.

At this writing, eight churches have been built in this style. Six are situated in locations where they are exposed to the views of many passing motorists. It is no wonder that the "A-frame," as laymen incorrectly call it, makes such a strong impression.

Although it is set back from Brockton Avenue so far that passing motorists may fail to notice it, the Hope Protestant Reformed Church — in the "A" style — is worthy of mention. It is the only one in town which was built by the members them-

"A"-Style Church Building (First Lutheran)

Assembly of God Church

selves. They dedicated it on Thanksgiving Day, 1983, after two years of labor.

Now we come to a peculiar trait in church congregations. They are the most conservative of our citizens but the most willing to experiment with radical architecture.

In Redlands, the foremost example is the First Assembly of God. With imagination and daring, the members in 1964 not only selected a hilltop site, they chose one that overlooks what was then the new freeway at Ford Street.

There, they built a church which is so different in style that you have to see it to understand how it looks. From the freeway you see no roof and no windows — only a very long stucco wall which rises higher and higher to the west, reaching a point. You might speculate that this is the home of a museum of modern art.

From the parking lot behind, however, you seem to be looking into a "V", the knave being in the center with wings on either side. On a Sunday morning the lot is chock full of cars — evidence of the Assembly's success in attracting members to this unusual location.

On the far side of the freeway-cut, the chapel of the Catholic El Carmelo Retreat perches on the ridge.

Back in the Central City, three of the large congregations began to itch for new churches. Fr. Henry Keane was able to make up his mind. Tear down old Sacred Heart — steeple and all — and rebuild on the historic Olive Avenue site. Architect Jerome Armstrong designed a church for the Catholics which is modern in feeling but traditional in profile.

Alas, the Presbyterians lacked such single-minded decisiveness. I am afraid that my friends of that faith suffer at times from an excess of democracy. They have a terrible time making up their minds.

One question was the site. Should they join the parade and march to the boondocks? They almost did. They bought property on Garden Street at Elizabeth, about a half-mile short of the Country Club.

On second thought, they decided to stay at Cajon and Vine,

where they set about acquiring still more property for parking and for future building.

Then they could not reach a consensus on the design for a new building.

At that juncture it may have been the Good Lord who intervened. In any case, the 1899 Sanctuary did burn down on that terrible night of June 29, 1967. Investigators never could pin the blame on an arsonist. They had to accept the probability that the conflagration was started by embers carried a block by the wind from the First Methodist Church at the Lord's Corner. That imposing edifice was also destroyed.

To complete this story, I should pause to say that the Presbyterian Church was somehow doomed to go up in flames. The building was only saved from destruction by valiant firemen on the night of February 3, 1939, when City Hall—just across Vine Street—went up in flames.

The phoenix that arose from the ashes was put into use in May 1970. Ultra-modern in exterior appearance, the new Presbyterian Church has an interior ambiance that makes old and young people feel at home.

Like their Presbyterian brethren, the First Methodists decided to rebuild from the ashes. Together with the Congregationalists and the Baptists, they would continue to anchor the Lord's Corner.

There is something about a fire which purges the mind. The Methodists retained no sentimentality for their picturesque church which had been a familiar sight for so many years. Instead, architect Leon Armantrout of Redlands designed a stark building of buff brick. Only the Cajon Street wall is broken by a window—a giant, darkish eye.

The only ornament is found in the afternoon when the sun casts sharp shadows of California fan palms on the Cajon Street wall.

Whether you like this building or not is a matter of personal taste. I'll leave the judgment to a couple of professionals, David Gebhard and Robert Winter in their guide book to architecture in Southern California. Their tight summation reads: "A contemporary brick-sheathed rectangular box; broken only by a large circular window facing onto Cajon; a very tasteful modern addition to Redlands' city center."

How far and how soon the influence of the Armantrout church will spread remains to be seen. In 1987, the town seems to have almost caught up with the need of the larger population for more church construction. The boom is probably over for a time.

For the Love of Old Houses

THE ELDERLY DOWAGER was condemned to die.

She was the elegant mansion of A. G. Hubbard on the Terrace. No one wanted her any more.

The Hubbards were all gone. So were the boys who attended a military school there. Now she was closing her final chapter, as a church. The members would leave when they completed the Highland Avenue Christian Reformed Church.

A developer planned to tear down the mansion and build a set of apartments on the cleared land.

The leading member of the congregation, John Van Mouwerik, came into the *Facts* office to plead with me as editor.

"Frank," he said, "Redlands ought to preserve that grand old lady. There's a lot of history tied up in her."

Indeed there was. At the east end of The Terrace the first church had been built. Hubbard, the fabulous mining millionaire, married the preacher's beautiful daughter. Near his home stood the first high school — the Hale Academy. At the west end of the street, residents of Lugonia had received their mail at the Lugonia post office, the first one in present day Redlands.

History? Yes, Redlanders had twice demonstrated their passion for it — the Golden Jubilee in 1938 and Surrey Days in 1948.

But preservation? No, not yet. John Van Mouwerik was a leader marching so far ahead of the band he couldn't hear the music. In fact, there was no music in 1961. Redlanders hadn't fallen in love with old houses; that would come later. By their silence, they let the mansion die.

Old houses? "They were the junk we lived in during the Depression and the War," a Redlander would exclaim if you asked him. "We didn't have the money to fix them up. We just slapped white paint on them and repaired the plumbing, the wiring and the leaky roof. Give me a new house with fuses that don't blow out, air conditioning, and a modern kitchen."

It was worse than that.

Even in the prosperous 1920s, various Redlanders were embarrassed by their picturesque but out-of-style Queen Annes. They would take off the gingerbread and surgically remove the turrets. A house that had been familiar to you might become almost unrecognizable.

It's no wonder that the owners wished to disguise their Victorian mansions. All across America they were being ridiculed in cartoons as the haunts of witches and ghosts.

Ironically, the sinister reputation of bulky old houses planted the slow-germinating seed of the Preservation Movement in Redlands. It happened this way.

In 1951 the MGM studio in Hollywood had in hand the scenario for *Talk About a Stranger*. The story called for a spooky house in an orange grove. Guessing that Redlands was a likely town, location scouts came here and "discovered" the Morey Mansion, on Terracina at Olive. The photographer, filming in black-and-white, could make the house look forboding by placing a dark filter over the lens of the camera.

Redlanders flocked to Terracina. Many movie fans went to get the autograph of George Murphy. Little did they guess he would later open the door from Hollywood to Washington, becoming a United States Senator in 1964. Ronald Reagan followed him on a similar route in 1981.

Nor did they appreciate just how quaint and just how picturesque David Morey's dream house really is. It would take more than MGM to open their eyes.

Six years later, in 1957, John Maass of Philadelphia published his spirited defense of old, maligned houses: *The Gingerbread Age — a View of Victorian America*. A native of Austria, he saw his new homeland with fresh vision. Enchanted by fanciful houses, he photographed, he painted, he published.

Some years later he said in a letter to me that of all the 100 photographs in his magnificent book, none had struck a more sensitive nerve than Morey.

Who could doubt the validity of his observation? The advertising agency for Carrier Air Conditioning made the Morey mansard roof and onion dome a virtual trademark. Graphic artists went wild. One of them even made a Christmas card in which Santa Claus is arriving with his sleigh and reindeer on snow-covered ground.

In the years ahead, Morey would attract scores of painters. You can find their pictures on the walls of countless Redlands homes. Leo Politi's version hangs in the A. K. Smiley Public Library and is reproduced on the dust jacket of his book, *Redlands, Impressions.*

Although this love affair with Victorians did not develop early enough to save Hubbard in 1961, it did inspire the compilation and publication of an influential brochure in 1963.

Redlanders love a Jubilee. "Historical Homes of Redlands" was a byproduct of "Celebrating 75 Years of Progress." Including the addresses and brief biographies of 93 houses, the publication made a hit.

Alas, it exposed a trap. The City then had no archives in which to verify supposedly correct information. We of the brochure committee learned a rude lesson. "If you want unreliable data on an historic house, just ask the typical owner."

Why is this so? Because we have no rule that he who builds a house must initiate a genealogy of it. Instead of a documented record, like the "family Bible," information — if any — passes from one owner to the next by word-of-mouth. Told and retold, these stories wander far from the truth.

While "Historical Homes of Redlands" did broaden the base of the slowly germinating Preservation Movement, it was the Prospect Park crisis that brought action.

Established in the latter 1890s by the England family of Philadelphia, "Prospect" is comprised of a large orange grove and winding carriage roads lined with ornamental trees. Like its larger and famous "cousin," Smiley Heights, it was visited by thousands of tourists in the railroad age and by three Presidents of the United States.

By 1963 housing tracts were sprawling all over town. It looked as if Prospect Park would be acquired by a subdivider. That put Redlands on the spot. "Preserve it now or lose it forever." That's the way it seemed at the time.

With optimism, the City Council asked the voters to authorize a bond issue to finance acquisition of the property. Although scores of leading citizens spoke or wrote in favor of the measure, 55 per cent of the ballots were cast against it.

Not all was lost. The campaign awakened many citizens to the reality that if cherished symbols of Redlands are to be saved, someone will have to put up the money.

Five years later Prospect Park was purchased for the City. Half the funds were contributed by generous citizens to match federal and state grants.

While the Prospect Park campaign provoked much preservation talk, something else began to register on the consciousness of the community. One landmark building after another disappeared.

Downtown, the process began in 1964. Arnholt Smith, San Diego financier, bought the whole block across from City Hall. He tore down everything, including the imposing Fisher Building, an historic testament to the importance of the business district. After excavating an enormous hole for underground parking, he decked it over and built the Redlands Plaza.

In June, 1967, two more landmarks met their fate. Fire destroyed the classic Presbyterian Church, just across Vine from City Hall, and the tall Methodist Church at Cajon and Olive.

When the Plymouth Village retirement community was developed on Cajon Street, upward from Palm, the picturesque Edwards Mansion, on the site, seemed to be a goner. Plymouth would give the haughty Victorian to anyone who would haul her away. Just when her case appeared hopeless, Don Wilcott stepped forward. He had movers cut her in two and haul her four miles to a site by Interstate 10, west of town. There she became a museum restaurant, celebrating the history of Redlands.

In 1974, the Redevelopment Agency began to clear the long-familiar buildings in Downtown, west from State, for the Mall. The Elks Clubhouse was razed. The 1914 Security Bank Building — a veritable Temple of Finance in Greek Revival style — fell to the wreckers.

But it was La Posada that somehow touched the soul of Redlands. Commanding the corner of Orange and State, the hotel had what Californians consider to be "Spanish" features, meaning white stucco walls and red tile roof. Never mind the blunt fact that such central city hotels were made obsolete by the motels conveniently located along the freeways. There are sentimental citizens who will insist until their dying days that "La Posada should have been saved."

While the vanishing landmarks played on the subconscious mind of Redlands, honor began to come to old houses that had long been taken for granted. The ladies of the YWCA envisioned annual house tours for the financial benefit of their organization. Their premiere, in 1975, demonstrated that people have an insatiable appetite for seeing how other people live in their homes. From then on, the YWCA tours were destined to return every year as regularly as the swallows to Capistrano.

The City did not have archives in which papers, pictures, maps and brochures could be collected, indexed and filed.

And history did not speak with a vibrant voice.

Both needs were met by one man.

Larry Burgess is a product of the Redlands schools and of the University of Redlands. Finding that history is his "thing," he went on to Claremont Graduate School. There, he wrote his master's thesis on the Smiley brothers. Fascinated by them, he further explored their lives while earning his Ph.D. The fruit of his scholarly research, in book form, is called: *As the Spirit Moved Them: The Smileys.*

With these credentials, he was a lucky catch for the A. K. Smiley Library. In 1972 he became the archivist, and in charge of special collections. Soon, he was appearing as a popular speaker on Redlands history before one audience after another. He had already begun to give classes in local history for adults. One of his students at the University of Redlands—Tom Atchley—was to become his colleague in adult education and his equal in a passion for digging into Redlands history.

Like the YWCA house tours, their classes have become a permanent fixture of community life. There are always some oldtimers who finally get around to taking the course. Newcomers who are anxious to learn about their adopted "home town," also enroll.

Students in the "Tom & Larry Show" find that Victorian houses are the visible link with Redlands history. Back of each Queen Anne stands the story of the pioneer who built it. Was he a ship's carpenter or a Yankee Bible thumper? Was she a doctor or the widow of a schoolmaster? Each biographical thread is woven into the fabric of the Redlands story.

As people learn more and more about local history, the more favorably inclined they become toward the older houses. That is the underlying strength of the Preservation Movement.

At City Hall, another Redlander became an important influence. He is Bill Schindler. For decades he was head of the Planning Department.

Bill wisely foresaw that if the movement was going to become strong it had to be built on a foundation of solid information. Generalities and mere emotion would not suffice.

In 1974 he initiated a program of identifying, describing and mapping the older houses. Bob Acheson pioneered the method and defined the task. Susan Fallows, also a student and a Redlander, followed a year later. She located 360 houses that were built before 1900.

Subsequent surveys have been conducted to the standards of the California Office of Historic Preservation, an agency that has made supporting grants.

In 1975 the Preservation Movement was gathering momentum. Ten houses, proudly owned and well kept, were selected for Heritage Awards by the Redlands Historical Society. In the *Facts* we published pictures of these homes as well as biographies of them. By 1983 my successor as editor of the newspaper, Terry Greenberg, would exclaim: "I've learned one thing. If it's about an old Redlands house—publish it!"

By 1975 a little joke of my own was beginning to have significant meaning for preservation. The house at 452 Cajon Street, built in 1892 and where I was born in 1912, had been torn down. With tongue in cheek, I would complain of the desecration and say that "instead of erecting a monument to the birthplace of The Great Frank Moore, they have put up an office for the Social Security Administration."

The point was that an investor had taken the only course permitted by City ordinance: tear down, build up. The old rule had become obsolete. At the behest of preservation-minded citizens the Council adopted a new ordinance which sanctions the conversion of old houses for non-residential uses.

The Adaptive Use Ordinance applies only to the Administra-

Victorian House adapted for office use
(440 Cajon Street)

tive and Professional Zone on Brookside Avenue, East Olive and Cajon Street. There, you will find a few conversions to offices—insurance, real estate, law and medicine. Up to this time the most conspicuous and pleasing rebirth of a Victorian house is The Learning Center at 440 Cajon Street.

My own fascination with old houses also began in 1975. I was a typical oldtimer. I had lived in Redlands all of my life without ever paying much attention to the houses as houses. Oh, yes! I did know many things—some nice, some scandalous, some amusing—about the people who had lived in them. But style? Almost nothing.

By consulting friendly architects, studying "house watcher" guide books, and inspecting residential districts from Nantucket to San Diego, I acquired a beginner's knowledge of historic houses. Soon, I was commenting on Redlands homes in the *Facts*—on Monday, perhaps, as columnist, and on Friday as editor. I like to think that appreciation of Redlands houses broadened and increased as a result.

By 1977, Redlands had become a place to go to see historic houses. *Westways* magazine advised motorists to "not miss Redlands as you speed along the freeway to Palm Springs." *Sunset* magazine gave a two-page layout to "Turn-of-the-century tour of Redlands . . . 60 handsome old residences." The text said: "Although Smiley Heights has long been subdivided, a surprising number of mansions—some of them splendid Victorians—remain." The *Los Angeles Times* Home section found vintage houses in Redlands to equal those in L.A.

From newspapers and magazines, Redlands moved into books. Terry Sillo, publishing *Excerpts from Southern California's Architectural Heritage,* wrote the sharpest captions. Sample: "Victorian railroad stations were important to the growing communities of Southern California. The station set the stage for the arriving visitor. When constructed in 1909, the Greek Revival Santa Fe station in Redlands, with its 311-foot-long promenade of columns, was symbolic of the thriving Redlands community and its growing civic pride."

Bringing out the second edition of their *Guide to Architecture in Los Angeles & Southern California* in 1977, David Gebhard and Robert Winter recanted. In 1964 one of them had still been under the spell of his professors of architecture who taught him to despise the likes of the Morey House. "Dishonest." "Meaningless ornament."

In 1977 they would write: "We have become older, perhaps more mature. Our taste has broadened. It is amusing to look back . . ."

They gave Redlands, full, sympathetic treatment — 32 things to see and a nice introduction: "Redlands has maintained its attractiveness, its sense of being separate and a very distinctive community."

Even such sophisticated groups as the Los Angeles Chapter of the Society of Architectural Historians came out to look over the town.

Members of the Historical Society began to feel their oats. They would not be content in the role of "the little old lady from Pasadena." They wanted Preservation to have clout.

All right. The Council would give them:

—An Historic and Scenic Preservation Commission to advise and recommend.

—A limited Preservation Ordinance so the Commission would have legal standing at City Hall.

The "Scenic" part came easily. A mere suggestion that the City might yank the California Fan Palms on some distant day and widen Cajon Street aroused the citizenry. The Council promptly gave blanket protection to four boulevards.

The "Preservation" part struck sparks. It was the Library. First, they stopped a contractor from sandblasting the walls and insisted on treatment that would not harm the bricks. Then it was the color — red or white? Views were passionately expressed. Adamant stands were taken.

This was more than the Council had bargained for. A motion to get rid of the Commission was defeated by only one vote.

Time heals.

The Council went on to:

—Add a chapter to the planning ordinances committing the City to a vigorous preservation program.

—Beef up the powers of the Commission with a stronger ordinance.

While Commissions No. 1 and No. 2 went about designating historic houses, private citizens were following their own bents.

Various couples fell in love with run-down Victorians, bought them, moved in, and slaved away. Curiously, after restoring their dream houses to their original glamour, most fixer-uppers sold them.

Johnny Moore took a squint at the unique McKenzie house on West State— stone walls at the first floor and brick at the second. He saw the making of a set of offices and converted the structure.

Phinney Building, Orange Street

With Henry Van Mouwerik, he dared to install a steel frame in the narrow, tall, brick Phinney Building on Orange Street. The derelict of 1892 attracted Joe Greensleeves elegant restaurant.

Wilmarth House, (214 W. Olive)

On East Olive Avenue, Bill Hardy, Jr. spotted the Lee Wilmarth Victorian, a small house with enough ornamentation to cover a mansion. When an authority on domestic architecture visited Redlands, he pretended he was seeing a Mark Twain-era steamboat. "My goodness!" he exclaimed. "It has everything but sidewheels." With costly renovation and remodeling, Wilmarth House became a set of offices currently occupied by a computer software company.

At the same time, something conspicuous was happening along some of the older streets. People began to discover that Victorians homes were not originally covered with just white lead paint. Oh, no! Grandfather and grandmother fancied lively colors.

Just as a woman's face can often be made more beautiful with lipstick, mascara and rouge, so does a house become more interesting when the features are brought out with paint.

The Simonds House on Olive at Alvarado had been plain white for years. Art Professor John Brownfield selected Wedgwood Blue to accent patterns, forms and ornaments. "Plain Jane" was tranformed into "Cinderella."

Simonds "Cinderella" House
(324 W. Olive)

While applying "make-up" to a facade may come rather easily, long-term preservation does not. Two locally famous houses have been in controversy for years. One is the striking Holt House, Olive at Alvarado, and the Burrage Mansion, overlooking West Crescent Avenue.

Preserving, restoring and improving Victorians costs a lot of money. Who can afford it? How can the owner make some income to offset his expenses?

During the mid-1980s aggressive and abrasive Jim Lotito made this a heated public issue. He occupied, but did not fully own, the Burrage house. While he lost the property he did provoke the City Council into adopting an ordinance permitting the bed-and-breakfast use of historic houses.

James Fishback Sr. bought the Burrage estate in 1987 and set about cleaning up the grounds and making the house livable.

How many couples will try to offer bed and breakfast? Will they find it profitable? Will they stick to it, or will they sell to another couple who, in turn, will find it too burdensome? These questions remain to be answered.

Fortunately, a few Victorians are preserved in mint condition by those who own, occupy and love them. Dr. and Mrs. Edmund Dombrowski maintain the 1905 Italianate mansion on Knoll Road in a way that would have delighted the builders, Mr. and Mrs. Oliver Hicks.

The picture book Queen Anne at 923 West Fern, built in 1890 by John P. Fisk, is owned by Dr. and Mrs. Larry Burgess. It is one of the few show houses that continues to have an authentic orange grove setting.

Fisk/Burgess House in Orange Grove
(923 W. Fern)

Kimberly Crest

Unique among the Heritage Houses is Kimberly Crest.

Conceived in the same spirit as Disneyland's Fantasy Castle, it stirs the imagination of children and adults, alike.

Perched atop a knoll just west of Prospect Park, the petite chateau looks down on a terrace, fountains, pergolas, lawns and trees. As any engaged girl can see, this is a romantic place in which to be married. Wedding follows wedding, from spring to fall.

When created by Mrs. John Alfred Kimberly in 1909, this was one of four Italian gardens in Redlands. Today, it is the only one that survives to give a dramatic setting to a mansion.

While the destinies of other Heritage Houses are in the hands of private owners, Kimberly Crest is entrusted to a perpetual corporation. Mrs. Elbert W. Shirk, daughter of Mr. and Mrs. Kimberly, made a bequest of it to the Kimberly Shirk Association—not to the City government—"for the enjoyment of the people of Redlands."

In a sea of uncertainty about the future of preservation houses in Redlands, Kimberly Crest stands as a model of stability. Somehow, some way, other cherished symbols of Redlands' history must be placed on enduring foundations. This can only come about with sustained effort by those who are dedicated to saving the heritage homes of this charming city.

To Stem the Urban Tide

BULLDOZERS PUSHED OVER the beautiful trees in still another orange grove on Citrus Avenue two miles east of town.

Redlanders winced as they drove by. Where would this desecration end?

Would the City—would the subdivider—spare the row of magnolia trees that stood between the pavement and the grove? The answer was only days in coming.

No, planning regulations required the subdivider to widen his side of Citrus Avenue, pave it and install curbs and gutters. These showy ornamentals promptly fell to a chain saw. The glossy leaves were heaped over the trunks and branches. The large, white blossoms of spring were but a memory.

That was it!

The slaughter of those familiar trees stirred a chord deep within people. More flocked to join The Friends of Redlands— the new and spontaneous movement to stem the urban tide.

Curiously, The Friends attracted as many newcomers as longtime residents. All of them shared a gut feeling that the town was being raped.

Indeed, Redlands was being swept by another tremendous boom. In the single year of 1977, the City issued as many building permits as in all the seven preceding years combined.

In June, 1977, The Friends announced their goals. They would "support rational and controlled growth which is consistent with the traditional character of Redlands."

"Control growth"? That was contrary to the belief in "progress" which had prevailed in Redlands from the earliest days. The idea had not been questioned much until 1963, the year of the first big boom of the post-War era in Redlands.

The Friends did not invent the policy which they proposed. Petaluma did. In 1972 that city, north of San Francisco, had grown in population by 25 per cent in two years. To avoid urban sprawl, the Council limited growth to 500 dwelling units per year for five years.

But does a municipality have the legal authority to control growth? That was a critical question upon which the future of regulation would depend throughout California.

In 1975 the Federal Ninth Circuit Court answered: "The concept of public welfare is sufficiently broad to uphold Petaluma's desire to preserve its small town character, its open spaces and low density of population, and to grow at an orderly and deliberate pace."

Yes, but what could citizens do if they favored growth control and the City Council did not?

They could turn to "Ballot Box Democracy." In Livermore they did. By an initiative measure in 1972, they suspended the issuance of building permits until new facilities could be built — school houses, water supplies and a bigger sewer system.

As in the Petaluma case, the opponents sued. The California Supreme Court found that the initiative ordinance reasonably related to the public welfare. The majority opinion, however, gave an implicit warning with this comment:

"Outsiders, searching for a place to live in the face of a growing shortage of adequate housing, and hoping to share in the perceived benefits of suburban life, may present a countervailing interest opposing barriers to immigration."

The attorney retained by The Friends got the message. An initiative ordinance would stand up in court if it sought to moderate growth; it would fail if it was too harsh.

As the month rolled on, The Friends organization grew in membership and in clout.

The Councilmen could not make up their minds about what to do. On November 1, 1977, they adopted a building moratorium. On November 4 they repealed it.

Fed up with this shilly-shallying, on November 25 the Friends published a legal notice of their intent to place a growth control initiative on the spring ballot.

Four days later the Council invoked a second moratorium, this time for 120 days.

The chaos subsided when the Council signed a contract with consultants to make an intensive analysis of the problems of growth control. Momentarily satisfied, The Friends suspended their plans to go to the ballot box.

While the study was being made with the participation of many interested citizens, it was just too slow. Anticipating the possibility of being stopped by an initiative, developers stepped up the pace. In June, 1978, they took out permits to built 532 dwelling units. That was more than the 12-month average for ten years. Patience ran out.

On July 14 The Friends filed petitions with sufficient signatures to qualify an initiative for the fall ballot.

The intent of Proposition R was well stated in the official title: an "Initiative ordinance to moderate the rate of growth within the city of Redlands to preserve the city's unique environment and character."

What rate of growth? For individually constructed homes, no regulation. For small apartments, no regulation. For "major subdivision residential development," 450 dwelling units per year. Included were "single family, multiple family, and mobile homes."

As you see, the target was bigness — big housing tracts and big apartment complexes.

The 450 limit would take care of the quantity of building, the sponsors thought, but what about quality?

Applications for the right to build residential subdivisions or apartment complexes would be competitively evaluated by at least eight criteria.

While the austere language of "Prop R," as it came to be called, provided the legal framework, the letters to the People's Column of the *Redlands Daily Facts* gave a better idea of what proponents had in mind.

One lady wrote: "Many of us who live here chose Redlands for its character, charm and uniqueness. We have stayed here even though, like my husband, they commute as much as one hundred miles to their jobs every day.

"This is basically a bedroom town, enriched by a fine university. Because of what Redlands has to offer it has always been a fine place in which to live.

"What a pity, if, over the years, it turns into another Anaheim."

Echoing her sentiment, a doctor added: "People who truly love Redlands want it to grow but don't want to lose sight of why Redlands is unique.

"I want my children to enjoy and love the Redlands I know, or should I say, 'knew'.

"What Proposition R really asks is: 'Will we remain special with our growth or will we become a suburb of Los Angeles?' "

Even the most emotional writers stopped short of saying what was in their innermost hearts. What they truly felt was that Redlands, swamped in an urban tide, would lose its very soul.

On November 8, 1978, the voters adopted "Prop R" by a landslide.

To win an election campaign was one thing. To implement the victory was another. It took months at City Hall to develop a point system for rating the applications for the opportunity to build.

Emerging as the foremost leader of the Friends of Redlands was an orthopedic surgeon, Dr. Kenneth Roth. He kept after the City Council to implement the initiative ordinance.

By 1980 he was the personification of Prop R. The voters elected him to the City Council. The Council elected him Mayor.

Also elected in 1980 was James W. Gorman, another Friends of Redlands stalwart. The new members, supported by long-term incumbent Charles DeMirjyn, had a majority.

But the Council era of the Friends lasted only four years. Gorman was defeated. Roth did not run for reelection. He found that being both a doctor and a councilman was just too much.

And now you are expecting a happy ending to this story. The dreams of the Friends of Redlands all came true, didn't they?

Wrong!

Prop R did not stem the urban tide.

It did not stop the cycle of boom and bust.

Builders became frightened. If a growth control law was adopted, they might be stopped, losing thousands of dollars they had invested in land and planning. The boom of 1977 became a building frenzy in 1978.

In those two years, permits were issued for 3,714 dwelling units. That boom was just twice as big as the previous one in 1963–64.

As in the past, a bust followed the boom. It lasted five years.

Then another two-year whopper came.

How, you are wondering, did Proposition R fail to moderate construction to a steady rate of 450 units per year?

The fundamental reality is that the City does not build houses, apartments or mobile home parks. The Council doesn't. The Planning Commission doesn't. Developers do.

In the main, developers build when they believe the market is right. They build as many units as they can finance and, hopefully, sell.

When the first boom collapsed, there were five straight years in which building never reached the 450-unit limit. The market was saturated. Developers either allowed their allocations of units to expire or kept them on hold while they waited for better times.

With a backlog of allocations they could use, developers again went wild in 1985–86.

The building of gigantic apartment complexes also began. This was amazing to The Friends as well as most other citizens.

What the Prop R authors probably did not realize in 1977 was that they chose to fight City Hall with a fragile weapon, an Initiative Ordinance.

Within a decade of their adoption, most state initiative measures approved by the voters are struck down by the courts, in whole or in part.

Proposition R, lawyers for a developer found, had a loophole which was so big that two gigantic apartment projects passed through it. The catch was the word "subdivision." Only projects on lands that were to be subdivided were under the growth control regulations. No subdivision was necessary for Parkview Terrace and Redlands Lawn and Tennis, both on Barton Road at Alabama.

Accepting the advice of the City Attorney, who said the developers were correct under the law, the Council surrendered. That was on August 25, 1985.

Outraged by this surprising turn of events — entirely contrary to the intent of Prop R — citizens returned to the ballot box on June 3, 1986. With an appropriate initiative, they plugged the loophole.

All of this is water under the bridge. Perhaps the allocation system needs more time in which to moderate growth. If it does, the long-term judgment on Prop R will be more favorable.

The measure will last long enough for this stock-taking.

Unlike the pioneering growth control schemes of Petaluma and Livermore, the Redlands Initiative has no provision for its own termination. Prop R will last until it is abolished by the voters, overruled by the courts or undercut by the Legislature.

What, then, of quality — of preserving the environment, the character of the town? Only one aspect is clear.

Prop R did not preserve the orange groves. It did not stop the clearing of the land.

Beyond that point there is no consensus. Opinions vary widely among well-informed people. There is no jury to render an independent verdict. Nor has the City hired a consulting firm to make an analysis — a sequel to the elaborate Growth Management Studies of 1978.

If a forum were conducted in the winter of this year, 1987, you would hear a discussion about like this:

Councilman (favoring R): The effect of R has been positive

because the applicants have been forced to meet quality standards to win allocations of dwelling units.

Consultant to builders: Some of the best builders of quality houses have been kept out of town because they cannot get an allocation of enough units at one time. The economics of their business limits them to fairly large tracts.

City Planner: There has been a marked improvement in the design of houses in recent years. They are better planned and more attractive in the eyes of the buyers.

Developer: In the past 15 years, builders have learned how to improve their products. Generally, a new project is better than the older one across the street.

Engineer: The market controls, not Prop R. Builders build what will sell. I know. I've talked to a lot of them.

Developer: One reason that houses are better now is that state law sets energy-efficiency standards which must be met. This means more insulation, more quality in construction.

Planner: Before Prop R, a developer built a tract in the University district with 40 houses, all alike. You don't see that happening now.

Also, if you look around you will notice that in nearly every new tract the developer landscapes the homes. They install lawn sprinklers. People have to stretch themselves to buy a home. If that takes all of the money they have, they may not landscape for a couple of years. With uniform landscaping, the subdivisions look better. Every homeowner is protected.

Our imaginary forum ends here.

The problem is that it is difficult, if not impossible, to isolate what might be called "The R Factor." If the effect is positive, do you give credit to "The Market" or to "R"? If it is negative, which do you blame? There are few impartial opinions.

As to the cost of houses, there are also many influences that determine the total. Before R, city building fees were modest. Now, they are not only big but numerous — schools, sewers, parks, water service and water capital improvements. One developer alleges that these fees amount to $10,000 to $12,000 for a single family dwelling.

There is no gainsaying the fact that the cost of houses has risen markedly since R was adopted. But various increases would still have occurred even if no growth control ordinance had been adopted. The question remains unanswered: "How much did the Initiative add to the cost of a typical house?"

In conclusion, a few words.

The quality of life was the real issue in the 1978 election. Many citizens felt that the urban tide, sweeping over Redlands, would destroy the qualities which they admire and love in this city.

The majority vote was in favor of a protection plan — Proposition R — but it was also a general statement of intent: "Don't let the developers determine the future of Redlands. We want the City government to take control."

In the long run, only part of the responsibility can be placed on City Hall. The quality of life which makes Redlands such a splendid place in which to live will only be maintained if the citizens themselves are devoted to preserving it.

The Smiley brothers taught Redlanders that a landscaped city attracts residents of the most desirable kind. It is up to each homeowner, then, to take pride in the appearance of his place.

When Mr. and Mrs. Clarence G. White gave the Prosellis, the magificent structure at the front of the Bowl, he said: "No city lives by taxes alone. The nearer it comes to that condition, the more drab and monotonous its existence is. Many of us take for granted the immense amount of free personal service that goes into making a town like Redlands.

"We hope that each man, woman, and child who has been impelled to do more for this community than he has been compelled to do will feel that he has contributed to the building of this Prosellis."

Robert Watchorn, donor of the Lincoln Shrine, showed us that good things come to a city that proves itself worthy of them.

Isaac Ford was wont to say that there will always be plenty of time to work for the good, for the beauty, of Redlands. We cannot live on the heritage from those who came before us. We must constantly renew and improve our city.

Proposition R can only deal with development of the land. The people, themselves, are responsible for the culture.

As citizens of the Redlands we love, our motto should be: "Community before self."

Index

REDLANDS – OUR TOWN
has been designed and printed in an edition of
3,000 softbound and 1,500 casebound copies
by The Castle Press in Pasadena.
It is set in Baskerville and Perpetua
typefaces and printed on archival
Warren's Olde Style paper.